Focus on

**Practical
Wine
Knowledge**

Focus on . . .
The Hospitality Industry
by Bruce H. Axler

Adding Eye Appeal to Foods
Breakfast Cookery
Building Care for Hospitality Operations
Buying and Using Convenience Foods
Increasing Lodging Revenues and Restaurant Checks
Practical Wine Knowledge
Profitable Catering
Room Care for Hotels and Motels
Security for Hotels, Motels, and Restaurants
Showmanship in the Dining Room
Tableservice Techniques

ITT Educational Publishing
Indianapolis · New York

Focus on . . .

Practical Wine Knowledge

by
Bruce H. Axler

Noted
Food Educator
and Consultant

ITT EDUCATIONAL
PUBLISHING
INDIANAPOLIS · NEW YORK

Practical Wine Knowledge

Library of Congress Catalog Card Number: 73-85984

International Standard Book Number: 0-672-26119-7

Printed in the United States of America

1. 9 8 7 6 5 4 3 2 1

Book design, cover design, and cover illustrations by Jorge Hernandez.
Text illustrations by William Blaney.

Contents

Perspective on Wine / **1**
    Introduction   1
    Sense, Common Sense, and Nonsense   2
    Grapes   3
    Overview of Wine Making   7
    Types of Wine   9

Guide to Purchasing Wine / **2**
    Wine Packaging   13
    Buying by the Label   16
    Price and Quality   29

Guidelines for Evaluation / **3**
    Procedure for Evaluation   31
    What to Look for in Evaluating Wine   35
    Knowing What to Expect in a
        Particular Wine   40

Guidelines for the Storage
   and the Care of Wine / **4**
    Personal Cellar Lists and
        Restaurant Wine Menus   47
    The Wine "Cellar"   51

Serving Wine / **5**
    Preparing Wine for Service   55
    Opening Wine Bottles   57
    Glassware   61
    Pouring Wine   61
    Formal or Restaurant Wine Service   62

Wine and the Menu   /   **6**
    Old Rules, New Rules, and No Rules   64
    Basics of Matching Food and Wine   67
    Guidelines for Personal Matches of
        Wine and Food   68

Wines of France   /   **7**
    Bordeaux   73
    Burgundy   83
    Champagne   90
    Rhône Valley   92
    Loire Valley   94
    Alsace   96

Wines of Italy   /   **8**
    Piedmont and Liguria   101
    Lombardy   103
    Veneto   103
    Trentino-Alto Adige and
        Friuli-Venezia Giulia   104
    Emilia-Romagna   105
    Tuscany   105
    Umbria and Latium   106
    Marches   106
    Abruzzi   107
    Campania, Lucania, Apulia, and
        Calabria   107
    Sicily and Sardinia   108

Wines of Germany   /   **9**
    Wine and the Law   118
    German Wine-Producing Regions   122

Wines of the United
  States and Other Countries   /   **10**
    Wines of the United States   126
    Other Wines of the World   131

Perspective on Wine

Introduction

If you've wanted to buy wine recently—or order it in a restaurant—you may have been faced with some dilemmas that have confronted many people at one time or another: Should you buy a white wine or a red wine? Is French wine better than German or Italian wines? What about domestic wines? How do you tell the difference if you're not an expert?

It doesn't matter whether you're a restaurateur buying wine by the case for use in your restaurant, or a member of the general public buying wine by the bottle for the boss who's coming to dinner or for the special family celebration. If you can't answer such questions yourself, you'll have to depend on someone else's word—probably a stranger's—and hope he knows what he's talking about.

Practical Wine Knowledge has been written to give you the answers to these and to more complex questions. It is a compilation of wine knowledge in an easily readable form, which makes this knowledge accessible and understandable to anyone who wishes to know more about wine.

Each of the three words in the title is important. *Practical Wine Knowledge* is down-to-earth and *practical;* it is about *wine;* and it will give you the *knowledge* you seek.

If you're a restaurateur, you're particularly interested in getting the best possible wine list to offer your customers at the best possible prices—and at the best possible profit. *Practical Wine Knowledge* will show you how. You want to stock a wide variety of wines, an acceptable range of choices for the diner. You don't want a list that offers only expensive wines, but you also don't want to insult the diner's palate. *Practical Wine Knowledge* offers guidelines that will help you buy a good, varied selection of wines within your budget requirements, with some choices to fit every type of customer—from the person who orders wine only on special occasions to the connoisseur who demands wine with every meal and demands the best.

If you're a consumer who simply wants to know more about wine in order to buy it more wisely— either for use in your home or when ordering it in a restaurant—*Practical Wine Knowledge* will give you the information you seek. If you're bewildered by the wide array of choices and prices that confront you, *Practical Wine Knowledge* will end that bewilderment with its useful, informative suggestions about purchasing wine, storing and caring for it, and serving it.

Sense, Common Sense, and Nonsense

An ocean of wine is available in the United States for the enjoyment of restaurant guests and consumers. In buying wine the restaurateur and the consumer are guided by two very different types of authorities: the traditional and the radical wine expert.

The *traditional wine expert,* in the person of a wine salesman, liquor store owner, or wine writer, would like to keep wine drinking a gentlemanly pursuit. He protects wine from the hoi polloi by investing it with a rococo ritualism. He enjoys wine knowledge as much as wine drinking.

The *radical wine expert,* who might be quite knowledgeable himself, argues that the pleasure of wine is never illuminated by experience or information, only overwhelmed. He advocates "know-nothing" wine drinking, with only "enjoyment" as a standard.

Somewhere between these two extreme positions there is surely a more reasonable approach: wine purchasing and wine drinking with information on a "need to know" basis. For example, knowing the pedigrees of wines which are virtually unobtainable is an academic exercise, but knowing which wines, among those available, offer a reasonable value for the money is nicely practical. By the same token, putting ice cubes in wine is neither sacrilegious nor a universally good idea; it's worth considering for *some* wines, *sometimes*.

Other such conundrums concerning wine service, wine-food combinations, wine storage, and wine tasting can have satisfactory resolutions if judgment is based on a few (not too many) hard facts. For instance, between the dogmatic prescription to "Drink red wine with red meat, and white wine with white meat" and the liberal permission to "Drink any wine with anything" there is an approach to menu planning that takes into account the prior experience and the diversity in tastes of a great many people for both wines and foods; for this approach, categorization of wine as "red" or "white" is inadequate.

Practical Wine Knowledge offers information, not romance—and guidance, not prescription. It is based on the premise that most people would prefer to understand what they are buying and to get the most out of every bottle they buy. Whether an individual's tastes ultimately lead him to wine blended with fruit juice or to Crusted Port is his own concern, so long as it is an honest fruit blend or a genuine Port.

Grapes

Most of the wine purchased and drunk in the United States is made from grapes. Only grape wine can be called *wine;* wines from other fruits must be qualified by the fruit's name: for example, "*cherry* wine."

TABLE 1.1. PRINCIPAL GRAPE VARIETIES

GRAPE NAME	GRAPE COLOR	WINE NAME	WINE COLOR	COUNTRY
Aligoté	White	Burgundy	White	France, California
Alvarelhão	Black	Port		Portugal
Barbera	Black	Barbera (Varietal)	Red	Italy (Piedmont) California
Bastardo (Trousseau in France)	Black	Port		Portugal, France (Jura)
Bouchet	Black	Saint-Emilion	Red	France (Bordeaux)
Boal	White	Madeira		Portugal (Madeira)
Cabernet-Sauvignon	Black	Saint-Emilion Médoc (Varietal)	Red	France (Bordeaux)
Canaiolo	Black	Chianti	Red	California Italy (Tuscany)
Chardonnay	White	Champagne Burgundy (Varietal)	White	France
Chenin Blanc	White	Vouvray Saumur (Varietal)	White	California France (Loire)
Furmint	White	Tokay	White	California Hungary
	Black	Beaujolais	Red	France (Burgundy)

Grape	Color	Wine	Color	Region
Gewürztraminer	White	"Spicy" Traminer	White	France (Alsace), Germany
Grenache	Black	Côtes-du-Rhône	Red	France
		Tavel rosé	Rosé	France
		(Varietal)	Rosé	California
Grignolino	Black	(Varietal)	Red	Italy (Piedmont)
		(Varietal)		California
Insolia	White	Marsala	White	Italy (Sicily)
Malbec	Black	Bordeaux	Red	France (Bordeaux)
Malvasia	White	Malmsey (Malvasia)	White	Italy (Tuscany, Lucania, especially Sicily)
		Madeira		Portugal (Madeira)
Merlot	Black	Bordeaux	Red	France (Bordeaux)
Mission	Black	Port		California
Muscadelle (used with other grapes)	White	Sauterne Barsac	White	France (Bordeaux)
Muscat	Black, White	Asti Spumante, Moscatel, Frontignan	Red White	Italy, France, California, etc.
Nebbiolo	Black	Barolo Barbaresco (Varietal)	Red	Italy (Piedmont, Lombardy, etc.)

GRAPE NAME	GRAPE COLOR	WINE NAME	WINE COLOR	COUNTRY
Pinot Blanc (Chardonnay)	White	Champagne Chablis	White	France
Pinot Noir	Black	Champagne Burgundy Varietal	White, Red	France (Champagne, Burgundy)
Rabigato	White	Port	White	Portugal
Riesling	White	Rhine Moselle Alsatian (Varietal)	White	France (Alsace) Germany Switzerland Austria, Chile, New York, California
Sangiovese	Red	Chianti	Red	Italy (Tuscany)
Sauvignon Blanc	White	Graves Sauterne (Varietal)	White	France (Bordeaux)
Sémillon	White	Sauterne	White	California France (Bordeaux)
Sercial	White	Madeira	White	Portugal (Madeira)
Traminer	White	Varietal	White	France (Alsace) Germany
Trebbiano	White	Chianti (Varietal)	White	Italy (Tuscany) California

The quality of the wine and 90 percent of its "character" depend on the variety, selection, planting, and cultivation of the grape from which it is made.

While the purchaser has little opportunity to determine much about the manufacture of a bottle of wine, the details of its transformation from grape to beverage and knowing from what grapes a wine is made will tell him something about the wine's taste. Wines made from the same grapes, while hardly identical, are in the same taste family. Put another way, part of the great difference between the Burgundy wines and Bordeaux wines of France (and between all their imitators) is in the use of Pinot grapes for Burgundies and Cabernet-Sauvignon grapes for most Bordeaux red wine. It might also be noted that many of the non-European wines are labeled by their grape varietal names. A California Grenache rosé, so labeled, will taste something like a French Tavel rosé, which also contains Grenache grapes.

The color of the grape is not necessarily the color of the wine, as both white and rosé wines may be made from black grapes. The taste of the wine will indicate the grape variety rather than the color, except in those wines, like Port, which are made in several varieties.

Overview of Wine Making

The basis of the "romance of wine" is the essentially inexplicable contribution to the qualities of the wine of the soil and microclimate of each grape-growing region, and, in the case of the great limited-production wines, the exact location of the region.

Cultivation of the vine bearing the grapes can influence the yield of wine and to some extent the quality of the product, but nothing can be done to change the wine's essential character, which is attributable to the marriage of vine and soil—a magic marriage in the case of good wines, an unhappy union in the case of average wines.

Vinification, or wine making, can have a greater influence. It may be impossible to create a great wine, but it is possible to ruin one. Wine is made from the juice of freshly picked grapes, either of a single variety or of several. The grapes are crushed, and almost immediately the first of two fermentations occurs: Yeasts (single-celled microscopic plants, present in the air and on the grapes) commence to convert the sugar in the grape juice to alcohol, water, and carbon dioxide. This fermentation, in casks or vats, may last two weeks.

Even by this point the vintner has engineered a great deal of the wine's quality. If the grapes picked were ripe or overripe, they are high in sugar and low in acid, and the grape juice (*must*) will also be high in sugar. If the skins have been left with the grapes, the wine will take on the astringent quality of the tannins they contain and may take on the color of black grapes.

Throughout the fermentation process, the vintner may control the temperature of the wine and thereby accelerate or decelerate the action of the yeast. The vintner may allow the fermentation process to go on until it finishes naturally; that is, when all the sugar has been converted, or when the alcoholic content is so high the yeasts no longer function. Or he may stop fermentation by adding chemicals, by regulating the temperature, or by adding alcohol (in the form of brandy), which has the effect of leaving some sugar in the finished wine. Later there is a second fermentation by bacteria which also takes place in casks or vats, except for Champagne and similar wines that are yeast-fermented for the second time *in the bottle*.

After the second fermentation, the wine is placed in storage casks or vats to age, or mature. The extent of aging is determined by the particular wine and the particular qualities of the grapes of that season. It may be a matter of a few weeks for some wines, or many years for others. At this point, the vintner's contribution is largely to leave the wine alone and, ultimately, to judge when it is ready for bottling. The most radical and distinctive changes occur during this storage period—not, as many individuals imagine, during further maturation in the bottle. Bottling largely stops the aging process; certainly bottling limits aging radically.

When the vintner has decided the wine in the cask is ready, that it has developed flavor, brilliance, and (hopefully) clarity, he bottles it, perhaps after clearing it chemically.

Prolonging the aging does not result in a continued improvement of the wine. Each wine has a definite peak in the cask, after which the wine declines. Likewise, there is no virtue in age, either in the cask or in the bottle: Wine X may be "excellent" in three years, and wine Y may be "excellent" in forty. Age as a standard of evaluation has meaning only in comparing bottles of Y of the same production year, drunk in different years.

In the bottle, the wine may be ready for drinking, or it may require further aging. Depending on the wine, a year, a decade, or a half century may be "right." The only way to tell is, first, by applying some precedent reasoning, to establish a threshold of acceptability based on the type of wine and the opinion of the growers. Historically certain wines are drunk "young"; others require long maturation; then, when this threshold has been established, the restaurateur can determine the wine's peak by tasting bottles periodically, or by following the taste experiments of a wine expert, either the purveyor or a wine writer. Then adjustments can be made for the expert's tastes.

Types of Wine

Distinguishing among wines is facilitated by classifying them according to certain of their characteristics. Any point of similarity between a known wine and an unknown wine is a step toward appreciating the unknown wine. Classification by country of origin, the method used in the second half of this book, while eminently suitable for logically and efficiently communicating information about a great many wines, cannot be made on the basis of an individual's *mental* categorization of wines. French wines as such, except for their country of origin, have nothing in common. A French Champagne has much more in common with a California Champagne than with a French claret. Four different systems offer more useful means of wine classification which can be further refined by those distinctions apparent from the labels (discussed in Chapter 2). These systems classify wines by use, by production method, by color, and by recognized "quality standard."

Wine Classification by Use

Apéritif wines are those specifically created to be drunk before a meal or as a "cocktail." They include spiced wines, such as vermouth, and various brand-name preparations, such as Dubonnet, Campari, Punt e Mes, and Lillet. Sherries and similar wines which may be drunk during a meal, but are not likely to be, are also included in this category.

Table wines are drunk with food, specifically with salty or spicy food. A table wine can be inexpensive or expensive, red or white (or a hundred other colors), still or sparkling. This category is certainly the largest.

Dessert wines are those that have sufficiently high sugar content so that they can be drunk with or after a sweet dessert. In general, as apéritifs they would blunt the appetite; with a salty main dish they would taste strange. Dessert wines can range from Sauterne to Port, a very wide range.

Refreshment wines are those created to be drunk

without food accompaniment, without even the antici-
pation of a meal. They are drunk instead of water,
milk, or punch, beer, fruit juice, or cola. Many of the
"new" American wines sold under upbeat brand names
and meant to be chilled ice cold or drunk on ice are
refreshment wines.

Classification by Production Method

While many refinements of production method are
not readily apparent, broad distinctions can be made
on this basis.

Natural wines are made by the simple fermentation
of grape juice, without the addition of alcohol or sugar
(beyond the very small amount of sugar which is allowed by law to supplement the natural sugar of some
wines in certain years). Natural wines are not made
sweet.

Fortified wines are wines that have had alcohol
added to them, sometimes with two results: a sweetness due to unfermented sugar present at the time
the added alcohol inhibited further activity by the
yeast, and an alcoholic content (or "proof") beyond
that of natural wine. A fortified wine may have 20
percent alcohol, in contrast to a natural table wine,
which does not exceed 14 percent alcohol.

Sparkling wines contain some carbonation. The
presence of carbon dioxide must always be induced by
a change in production method, whether the carbonation is as light as the few bubbles in a French Vouvray,
or as heavy as the supercharging of an artificially
carbonated "new" wine.

Made wines are blends of wines, or of wines and
other natural or artificial products to meet a brand
standard. These are wine cocktails of which the best
Champagnes are the most notable examples, and South
African brand-name drinks that combine cola syrup,
brandy, and red wine are the most dramatic.

Classification by Color

Color can be a very meaningful distinction between wines, or one without value. There are two problems: (1) wines are not neatly red or neatly white; they are every conceivable color that could be loosely construed as red or white, from purple to green; (2) a categorization on this basis is dangerous because it sometimes occasions the presumption that there is something a red wine can do that a white wine cannot.

The distinction is good when it communicates a great many other distinctions. For example, white Graves is a very famous and often very expensive wine, for reasons that have nothing to do with color; red Graves is less well known and a totally different type of wine. Color would be an important distinction were a merchant offering cases of Graves. Likewise white Port might be distinguished from Ruby Port, or white Chianti from Chianti.

Classification by Recognized "Quality Standard"

Major European producers, namely France, Italy, and Germany, award designations of relative merit to wines which meet certain standards of quality and genuineness as presented. Although the variation within these categories is tremendous, literally from very ordinary wines to transcendent wines, the words *Denominazione di Origine Controllata* on an Italian wine or *Appellation Contrôlée* on a French wine mean that the wine is genuine, that it is produced in the region the label indicates in the year indicated, etc. By extension, it means that the wine has a certain quality, although these designations are not ostensibly for that purpose. There is little point in protecting totally indifferent, unwanted wine.

The Germans are much more explicit; for example, the *Qualitätswein mit Prädikat* are quality wines (another designation) with special attributes.

Guide to
Purchasing
Wine

In purchasing wine, the individual consumer or restaurateur may have an abundance of choice and an ample arena for judgment and evaluation, or he may have the most limited selection.

Aside from considerations of taste or price, the purchase of wine is controlled by law. Various federal regulations govern the importation of wine, and the laws of fifty independent states govern its sale. Innumerable counties and municipalities restrict its purchase, some to the point of prohibiting it.

Some restaurateurs cannot sell wine; others cannot sell it by the glass. Others can buy it in the bottle but not in the cask.

The price may be fixed, supported by a minimum markup, or not fixed at all. The extent and type of taxation is also an important price factor; taxes, and their forms, vary throughout the country.

In many instances the restaurateur and the consumer shop for quality and value, not for price or variety. The object of the prudent purchaser is to get what he pays for.

Wine Packaging

The largest bottle that the individual consumer or restaurateur is likely to encounter is the magnum, equivalent to two bottles (52 ounces), and the smallest is the nip or baby of Champagne (6 to 6½ ounces). There are larger bottles, but they are seldom-seen

TABLE 2.1. BOTTLE SIZES

NAME OF BOTTLE	CAPACITY (ounces)	USED FOR
Nip, baby, split	6–6½	Champagne, sparkling wines
Split	8	Dinner wines, Chianti
Half bottle	12–13	Dinner wines, Champagne
Half bottle (tenth)	12.8	Refreshment wines, dinner wines, apéritifs (Sherry, Port)
Pint	16	Refreshment wines, Sherry, Port, muscatel
Imperial pint	18	Champagne
Bottles	24–26	Wines of all types
Fifth (⅘ quart)	25.6	Wines of all types
Bottle	30	Chianti, vermouth
Quart	32	Wines of all types
Magnum	52	Used occasionally, dinner wines, Champagne
Half gallon	64	Wines of all types
Gallon	128	Wines of all types

curiosities. Most commercial bottles fall between these two extremes. Exact contents must be stated on the label.

There is some relation between the size of the bottle and the quality of the wine it contains. The standard bottle with a cork is the most common for quality wines. If the same wine is put into a small bottle it will mature more quickly; in a magnum, more slowly. Wines in bottles with screw cap closures, or flat mushroom corks, will not mature in the bottle, whether the wine is an expensive Sherry or a gallon of an inexpensive refreshment wine.

The shape of the bottle is some indication of the wine it contains; that is, some wines are packaged in characteristic bottles.

Wine can also be purchased, both here and abroad, in other containers. Cans, similar in all respects to soft-drink cans, will undoubtedly become more widespread, especially for cask-aged wines and refreshment wines. Plastic bottles and flexible heavy plastic sacks are also coming into use.

The type of bottling can be an important purchasing consideration. The cost of bottling, shipping, and handling a bottle of inexpensive wine is the same as the cost for an expensive wine. When the buyer purchases the inexpensive wine in a bottle, a large percentage of his money, perhaps 80 to 85 percent, is for packaging. As the price of the wine increases, the fixed costs remain the same, and the percentage for packaging decreases. Since the percentage for packaging the inexpensive wine is so high, a small change in the selling price of the wine means a considerable percentage increase that can be spent by the merchant on the wine. For example, 80 percent of $2.00 is $1.60, the packaging cost, leaving 40 cents for the wine. When the price of the wine is increased 25 percent to $2.50, and the packaging cost remains constant, there is 90 cents to be spent on the wine, an increase of 225 per-

Figure 2.1. Some wines are packaged in characteristic bottles. *Top:* Bottles for Bordeaux and French vermouth. *Bottom:* Bottles for Chianti, Champagne, Burgundy, Rhine or Moselle, and Steinwein (this bottle is called Bocksbeutel).

cent. The merchant can then spend more than twice the amount on wine.

Essentially, this argument demonstrates two points: (1) inexpensive wines are better bargains in large containers; and (2) inexpensive wines in bottles may not be bargains at all, since a relatively small sum more *can* buy a much better wine.

Buying by the Label

There is a difference between buying a bottle of wine and buying a can of peas by the information on the label. Although there is less information on the can of peas, the label tells most of what there is to know about the peas and leaves little to interpretation. The wine label has more information, but only part of the information can be the direct basis for a purchase; the rest must be interpreted. The wine label also leaves essential questions unanswered; most important, "Is the wine any good?"

After such objective factors as the color of the wine and the number of ounces in the container have been considered, the purchaser may encounter as many as 20 items of information that are meaningful only if he can interpret and understand. For example, to someone who hates Brouilly or loves Brouilly or simply knows what it is, the word on the label is the basis for a judgment.

In large part, for an unknown wine, the label helps only to formulate some important questions to be answered, either by research (perhaps in the second half of this book) or by experimentation. Otherwise, the label offers a series of clues to the quality and character of the wine; some of them are sufficiently significant to influence a decision to buy or not to buy the wine. Often as many as 22 types of information may appear on a bottle:

1 Name of the wine
2 Country of origin
3 Color
4 Year grapes were crushed
5 Region where grapes were grown and crushed
6 Kind of wine
7 Percentage of alcohol
8 Liquid ounces bottle contains
9 Official and governmental guarantees
10 Place where wine was bottled
11 Trademarks
12 Shipper's name
13 Importer's name
14 Liquor store name or distributor name

15   Grape variety
16   Diplomas, certificates, and classifications
17   Ingredients added to the grape juice or wine
18   Advertising messages, illustrations, mottos, or claims
19   Product information
20   Corporate name of the wine's producer
21   Marks descriptive of quality
22   Sugar content of grapes or sweetness of the wine

Only the name of wine (or kind), the percentage of alcohol, the bottler, and place where the grapes were grown and crushed is mandatory on all wines.

Most of this information, when it appears, is on the main label of the bottle. However, some of it may appear on a seal affixed to the capsule of foil or plastic covering the cork, on a neck label, or on a back label.

1   Name of the Wine

The name on the wine label can identify the wine in the bottle as surely as a driver's license identifies an individual; or the name may mean very little. If the label were to show Château Mouton-Rothschild as the name of the wine, almost the whole story is told: there is only one Mouton-Rothschild. On the other hand, if the bottle says Liebfraumilch, which is a legitimate but invented name, little is learned: almost any German Rhine wine can be in the bottle. Between these two extremes are several different kinds of names which offer different degrees of information.

Geographical names, which would include Mouton-Rothschild and all the other estates and vineyards in Germany, France, Italy, and the United States that give their names to the wines they produce, become more meaningful as they refer to smaller and smaller areas. Mouton-Rothschild, for instance, may be identified by a series of geographical names, each with fewer referents: French wine, Bordeaux, Médoc, Pauillac, Château Mouton-Rothschild. The geographical names have descended from a country to a tiny plot of land.

When large areas, countries, and whole growing regions are on the label, little information is given. The middle ground offers more information but can be misleading. For example, Champagne, Burgundy, and Sauternes are places in France. Names like California Champagne, Chilean Burgundy, and Spanish Sauterne mean very little. Perhaps somebody in one of these areas thinks he has a wine that resembles the wine from these places, or he would like the customer to think so.

French wines, when they are guaranteed as to origin by the government (discussed below), come from a precise geographical location. On the other hand, German wines and Italian wines, even when they have similar guarantees, may not. The German law prior to 1971 permitted a producer to use a name taken from any place within a 15-kilometer radius. Understandably, growers tend to use the most famous and successful name they can.

Varietal names indicate that the wines contain a certain variety of grape. There is a good deal of information in the name, provided the customer is familiar with the grape from experiencing another wine and that the variety of grape, as named, is not misleading. For example, someone who knows that Beaujolais contains Gamay grapes will not recognize the California Gamay he bought on that basis.

Generic names are often place names so widely used, away from the actual location, that they have a supposed identity all their own: Sherry, Madeira, Port, Burgundy. Unfortunately, little faith can be placed in a generic name, because its definition is too encompassing. If Sherry is defined as a sweetish high-proof wine with a nutty cooked flavor, then all sweetish high-proof wines with a nutty cooked flavor are Sherry. They are not.

Brand names can tell the entire story, or very much of it. Bottles of Bristol Cream or Dry Sack Sherries, produced by Harvey and Williams & Humbert respectively, are as surely those wines as a brand-name coffee is that brand.

Brand names of Champagne like Bollinger, Krug, Perrier-Jouet, and Taittinger need very little further qualification (qualities within the brand, vintages) to mean exact wines.

2   Country of Origin

The name of the country of origin qualifying a generic name can tell the purchaser a great deal. A Sauterne in France is grown in a specific region, from a certain grape, by a specific method of cultivation, under controlled yield per acre, etc. Sauterne in California may be grown under as rigorous but different regulations.

Country of origin, in that it tells the buyer that the wine must be imported, also tells him that it was transported over great distances; considerable handling and import taxes have been included in the price.

3   Color

Sometimes the bottle will state the color of the wine as "red" or "white," which is useful information when the pale or dark relative of some famous wine is being considered. The white Beaujolais or the red Graves may be a bargain, but not if red Beaujolais or white Graves is used as the standard.

4   Year the Grapes Were Crushed

Wine labels or a separate label may have a year printed on them. This indicates that most of the grapes used in the wine were produced in that year.

It can mean much more. It can mean that in the

opinion of the producer, and of professional or government evaluators, that that year was a *vintage* year. The wine is a product of a season that produced excellent grapes from which first-quality wine was made. When the year is poor, the particular producer may choose to skip a year. All the wine produced, even when made entirely of the grapes of one year, may be offered without an indication of the year. In some cases, the producer, usually of extremely prestigious wines, may not even offer the wine under the estate or vineyard name. He may sell it with only a geographical name.

Unless the year on the bottle indicates a true vintage, its presence means very little. German wines, for example, have a "vintage" every year; it is no indication of quality. A bottle of wine with a year on it, without the year being a vintage year for that particular wine, is probably priced somewhat higher than a comparable nonvintage wine. The nonvintage wine may be better if skilled professionals have blended a wine of several different seasons' production to make up for the deficiencies of the wine of the particular season. Vintage charts which treat every year by region are unfair to many wines within the region; they are necessarily colossal generalizations. Also, they tend to incease the price of bottles labeled with the year in high-rated years, thereby creating bargains of the nonvintage wines of that period and of the good wines in supposedly bad years.

5   Region Where the Grapes Were Grown and Crushed

An indication of the region where the grapes were grown and crushed qualifies any generic or varietal name. California Sherry is not New York Sherry, nor is California Riesling the same as New York Riesling.

6   Kind of Wine

The label may indicate that the wine is table wine, dessert wine, apéritif wine, fortified wine, special natural wine (mixed with fruit juice), carbonated wine, sparkling wine, et al.

7   Percentage of Alcohol

The alcohol content of the wine is given as a percentage on bottles of wine. On bottles of spirits, it appears as a "proof" equal to twice the percentage (12 percent equals 24 proof). Apéritif wines and Sherries have between 17 and 20 percent alcohol; table wines, between 10 and 14 percent; dessert wines, between 14 and 21 percent.

8   Liquid Ounces

The exact contents of the bottle will be stated. Although this is obvious in standard bottles of wine, a fifth may look like a quart, and exotic bottles may contain less than they seem to hold.

9   Official and Governmental Guarantees

Some wines have a potential market that far exceeds the production capacities of the region that produces the wine. In order to guarantee that the wine in the bottle is properly represented, the governments of several producing countries, notably France, Germany, and Italy, guarantee the origin of the wine as to place of production. To some extent they also guarantee that the wine meets certain standards to merit the guarantee. For example, in France, where regulations are strict and well enforced, there are three *Appellations d'Origine*, which in addition to guaranteeing origin are tantamount to broad ratings. *Appellation Contrôlée* is the highest grade, to which almost all great French wines belong. The others are *Vins Délimités de Qualité Supérieure* (V.D.Q.S.) and *Appellation Simple*, which are seldom exported.

On a wine label the name of the wine may be followed by the words *Appellation Contrôlée*, or by a phrase with these words bracketing a geographical name; for example, *Appellation Pauillac Contrôlée*. The smaller the region named in the middle, the better the control.

The Italian wine law is similar. When the words *Denominazione di Origine Controllata* appear on a wine label, the wine is certified as to place of origin, grapes used, planting of vines, etc. There is also a category above this one, *Denominazione di Origine Controllata e Garantia,* which is a quality standard given to selected wines that already merit *Denominazione di Origine Controllata.* The Italian system, unlike the French, is a recent development.

German wine law is even more recent. The 1971 bottles, which arrived in the United States in 1972, were the first to which it applied. Germany had long relied on its fraud legislation to protect its established vineyards.

There are three categories of German wine:

1 *Deutscher Tafelwein* ("German table wine"), which must be produced from approved grape varieties in one of five major table wine regions: Mosel, Rhein, Main, Neckar, or Oberhein. No vineyard name appears on these bottles.

2 *Deutscher Qualitätswein bestimmter Anbaugebiete* (QBA) ("German quality wine of designated regions"), which must be made of approved grape varieties, has at least 7 percent alcohol and comes exclusively from one of the 11 quality German wine regions. Every bottle carries a control number showing that it has been tasted and analyzed to ensure that it is worthy of the label. It can be labeled by the region, subregion, or vineyard in connection with the name of a village. To use its name on a label, a vineyard must be at least 2.5 acres in size; this eliminates 23,000 to 24,000 vineyards and simplifies the understanding of German wine labels.

3 *Deutscher Qualitätswein mit Prädikat* ("German

quality wine with special attributes") is the highest category of German wine. It is made from approved grape varieties and contains at least 9 to 10 percent alcohol without sugar added. Within this category several subcategories, the attributes (*Prädikats*) are indicated on wine labels:

Kabinett ("cabinet") wines must be made from fully mature grapes and have a fruity quality.

Spätlese ("late harvest") wines are made from grapes picked after the completion of the normal harvest, when they are more mature. These wines have a richer taste.

Auslese ("selected harvest") wines are made from the ripest bunches of grapes and are individually selected and pressed. Some of them have the noble rot (*edelfäule*, or *Botrytis cinerea*), which concentrates their juice and sweetness.

Beerenauslese wines are made from grapes harvested individually.

Trockenbeerenauslese wines are made from noble rot grapes harvested individually.

Eiswein is made from grapes which have been frozen during the harvest and pressing.

10 Place Where Wine Was Bottled

Wine need not be bottled where it was made, any more than grapes need be pressed where they were grown. Some wines are sold to shippers in casks where they are aged and sometimes blended before being bottled under the shippers' control. Many less expensive wines in world commerce are transported in tanker ships, like oil, and pumped from place to place. Even some quality wines are moved in 600- to 700-gallon vats.

There is a premium price attached to the words "estate bottled," or the equivalent: *Mis en Bouteilles au Château* or *au Domaine* or *originalabfüllung*. This is a guarantee that the wine has been controlled throughout its making by the property that produced it. The question is really whether that alone is a guarantee of any particular quality standard. If the wine is nonvintage, for example, the blend of several years, it is entirely possible to argue that an experienced shipper/bottler might be a better blender. Sometimes the production of a wine is so large that the vineyard cannot handle the bottling: the identical wine can be sold at two prices on this basis.

The English have had a long tradition of importing wines in casks and bottling them in England. This has resulted in cheaper wines for the English customer, and often superior products have been saved from mediocrity by experienced cellarmen who know how to treat a sick wine.

11   Trademarks

Many wine names are trademarked—that is, protected against exploitation by other firms. Devices, insignia, art, and indeed the entire label may also be protected. Trademarks, however, do not reflect the quality of the wine, no matter how elegant they appear or how grandiose they sound.

12   Shipper's Name

Shippers specialize in a quality of wine. The shipper's name on a product indicates that the wine meets its standards. It is possible for the wine purchaser to "follow" certain shippers.

13   Importer's Name

Although in the United States the importer does not have the role of the English wine merchant, most importers offer a somewhat consistent variety of wines.

They import for their own market. Certain houses offer consistently good wines.

14   Liquor Store Name or Distributor Name

Certain liquor stores in urban areas and distributors trading with restaurants have become skilled specialists in wines. Their names at the very least mean that the wines they offer have been properly taken care of. Probably they also employ knowledgeable individuals. The local liquor store or the general spirit distributor, however amiable, is probably not so good a source as one of these specialists.

15   Grape Variety

Even when wine is not named after a grape variety, the label may indicate that the wine is made from a specific kind. Since the producer has no obligation to supply this information, the grape name on the label should be taken as a positive indication. Wine producers do not seem so sophisticated in this matter as other manufacturers whose advertising highlights and applauds common practice.

16   Diplomas, Certificates, and Classifications

On some wine labels appear representations of medals won in contests or at fairs. These can be disregarded, for a success of a hundred years ago is largely irrelevant; each year there is a new wine.

There have been efforts at certification of wine, for example, by the Association for the Development of the Exportation of Bordeaux wine (A.D.E.B.). This certification may appear on the wine label. (The A.D.E.B. used a seal on the capsule.)

One system of classification and certification does prevail for some of the great Bordeaux wines. Some wines were classified in 1855, others in 1953, and still others in 1955. Some Bordeaux wines comparable to those classified (the Pomerols) have not been classified.

The ranking wines in these classifications display their class: for example, Château Latour is a *grand cru classe*.

17 Added Ingredients

When fruit juice or spices have been added to a wine, the addition must be noted on the label. When sugar is sometimes added to the must produced in cold seasons to bring it to sugar levels which will produce a normal alcoholic content, no note is made on the label. Sometimes the absence of additional sugar is noted on German wines, by an indication that the wine is natural (*naturwein, naturrein,* or *ungezuckert*). The most recent legislation restricts the practice, which is limited in any case to the cheaper German wines.

In California sugaring is never necessary. In New York State it is sometimes "necessary" to add both water and sugar to the must to increase the alcoholic content and to reduce the acidity. This is not noted on the label.

18 Advertising Messages, Illustrations, Mottos, and Claims

A producer or shipper can place any advertising message he wants on a label. Although subject to the fraud legislation of the areas in which the wine is produced or sold, he can still praise his product extravagantly. For example, any wine may be called a great wine or *grand vin*. Other terms that may have some meaning are not rigidly enforceable; for example, *première cuvée* means the wine is among the best in an area, but it might easily be confused with *Premier Cru*, a classification that is rigidly controlled.

There is a good deal of "quality by association" promulgated by wine labels. For example, château bottling (*see* section 10 above) is a selling point, indicated on wine bottles by some phrase on the order of *Mis en Bouteilles au Domaine*. Other similar phrases appear on labels when in fact the wine was bottled away from the place where the grapes were grown. For example, *Mis en Bouteilles dans nos Caves, Mis en Bouteilles dans nos Chais*, and *Mis en Bouteilles à Fuisse* mean that the wine was *not* bottled at an estate. In one instance, a wine was bottled at another château and this fact was proudly proclaimed.

The reputation of the great Bordeaux estates, enforced by a system of classification, has encouraged producers in other areas to dignify their labels with a picture of a castle. Even in Burgundy, wines which have the name of a particular château exploit this association, when in fact there is no classification of Burgundy châteaux and other words in smaller type on the label are more important, specifically the vineyard area.

Sometimes, actual names are exploited by near spellings; for example, Château Lafite has occasioned some La*ff*ites and La*fitt*es.

19 Product Information

Product information can be sound advice on how to serve the wine—for example, well chilled. The producer may also choose to discuss such matters as the location of the vineyard, the history of the area and the wine, famous people who have enjoyed the wine, or his family.

20 Corporate Name of the Wine's Producer

The label tells the purchaser what company owns the property on which the wine was grown and produced. This is obvious on American wine labels but somewhat less clear to us when written in French, Italian, or German. On French labels, for example, the abbreviation *Ets.* (for establishment) indicates the company. *S.A.* on French, Italian, and Spanish labels is the equivalent of "incorporated."

21   Marks Descriptive of Quality

Sometimes wines, like Cognac brandies, are labeled with initials which may have some meaning; for example, Marsala wine may have the letters C.O.M. (Choice Old Marsala) or S.O.M. (Superior Old Marsala). On French wines, a virtually meaningless C.E. (*cuvée extra*) may appear.

22   Sugar Content of Grapes or Wine

In addition to the German wine terms discussed in section 9 above, Champagne is another notable example of a wine's sweetness being indicated on the bottle.

When Champagne is being recorked after a second fermentation has taken place in the bottle (to give it the bubbles), a small amount of sugar syrup and wine is added to replace the sediment from the second fermentation, which has been removed.

The quantity of sugar syrup determines the sweetness of the wine. This is indicated on the bottle. *Brut* indicates up to 1½ percent, *Extra Dry* up to 3 percent, *Dry* or *Sec* to 4 percent or 5 percent or more. The words *Goût Anglais, Goût Américain,* and *Goût Français,* after the major markets for Champagnes of varying sweetness, correspond to *Brut, Extra Dry,* and *Sec* respectively.

Price and Quality

In buying wine, the purchaser gets exactly what he pays for. When he buys a great bottle for a substantial price, he gets his money's worth. When he buys a mediocre wine in an outlandish bottle, he gets his money's worth. The purchaser does not buy only the liquid in the bottle—that much wine, that much glass, and that much cork. He buys a reputation, real or fancied, deserved or unmerited. The greater the reputation, the greater scarcity of the wine, the greater the demand for it, the greater the price. No one can seriously believe that one wine is worth a hundred or two hundred times another, except on this basis. The cost of manufacturing, bottling, merchandising, and shipping a great bottle, with the exception of the specially harvested German wines, is almost the same as the cost for a very inexpensive wine.

The bargains in wines are those which do not have the reputation of the higher priced wines discussed in sections 9 and 14, but have quality and character to commend them. The bargains in the French wines bearing an Appellation d'Origine are surely among the V.D.Q.S. wines which are not yet "in." The bargains in the Bordeaux wines are those which have not been classed or are classed below the well-known *crus:* for example, the wines classed *Crus Bourgeois Supérieurs* and *Crus Bourgeois.*

Certain wines are definitely nonbargains. Inexpensive French, German, Italian, Spanish, and Portuguese wines have to be transported great distances, handled by innumerable middlemen, and taxed by the federal government before they can be sold. How much of the few dollars they bring can be paying for the wine? On the other hand, a California wine in a jug has a much lower overhead per ounce. Chances are that some of the difference has been spent on the wine.

Guidelines for
Evaluation .

It would be false and arbitrary to suggest that one wine is "better" than another. Fair value, a dollar's worth of wine for a dollar in the opinion of the purchaser, is the only truly universal standard that can be proposed. On the other hand, objectivity in matters of taste cannot lead to the conclusion that every wine is the same. Wines have remarkably different qualities. Evaluation for purchase requires (1) knowing what to look for in wines and (2) knowing what to expect of the particular wine.

By knowing what to look for, the purchaser can establish some bench marks for evaluation. For example, the color of the wine is an important aspect of its quality. Every evaluation should include a consideration of the wine's color, although there is no "right" color for wine.

By knowing what to expect of a particular wine, the purchaser can effectively apply a set of standards. For example, the purchaser may know that a certain wine is usually garnet red; if it appears bluish red he knows that it has probably been adulterated.

Procedure for Evaluation

The circumstances for tasting a wine with evaluation in mind can depart significantly from the circumstances in wich the wine will be enjoyed. An evaluation is a test, and the purchaser must create a situation in which the wine's qualities will be evident, neither unfairly obscured nor subtly bolstered.

Selecting Wines for Evaluation

When the individual consumer or the restaurateur is evaluating wines for purchase, he may be able to attend a complimentary tasting arranged by a purveyor, importer, or wine society, or he may need to purchase the wines in order to evaluate them.

In either case, the wines tasted at a particular session should be related so that each wine's particular qualities are sharply focused. It is best to avoid dramatic contrasts; these are often unfair to the wines tasted later in the session.

Even when the wines are related, it is wise to taste them in an order that minimizes the influence of the wine tasted first. Tasting inexpensive wines before expensive wines, young wines before mature wines, and dry wines before sweet wines, regardless of color, protects the taster's objectivity.

Most purchasers will find it very difficult to evaluate more than six or seven wines in a single session.

Physical Circumstances of the Evaluation

It is very important that the circumstances of the tasting not intrude on the evaluation. Ideally, the evaluation should take place in a modest room, lighted by daylight, with a temperature of 68 degrees F and a humidity of 50 percent. Obviously, a marvelously contrived cellar scene can lend a very ordinary wine credentials it does not deserve. Daylight shows wine as it really is; normal incandescent light is acceptable, but colored lights and fluorescent lights distort a wine's appearance. The temperature and humidity of the room affect the taster's abilities and can prejudice him. A very light, well-chilled wine may appear extraordinary in a hot room, while an excellent heavy red may only add to the taster's discomfort.

A white cloth or sheet of paper should be provided for proper color evaluation; a candle or weak light bulb permits an examination of clarity.

The taster should also be aware of his own immediate physical condition as a potential influence. For example, head colds and allergy attacks severely distort taste perception, sometimes making it sensitive to particular qualities, sometimes making it completely insensitive.

Although habitual smoking has no effect on the ability to judge wines by taste—many wine experts and professional buyers smoke—smoking while tasting distorts taste perception. If the purchaser smokes all the time while tasting, the practice is acceptable. In fact, it may be necessary, as the taster's memory of various wines may include the taste of the smoke.

Unless only one or two wines are being evaluated, some facility should be provided for spitting the wines as they are tasted: a box of sand, a bucket, or a spittoon. Alcohol influences judgment and taste.

The evaluator also should beware of conditioning his taste ability during the tasting or just prior to the tasting by eating foods like cheese, which will make the wine taste exceptionally good, or foods such as fruit, which may make certain wines taste bad.

Condition of the Wine

Wines being tasted should be offered in a condition similar to that in which they will normally be served. Briefly, because Chapter 5 discusses this matter in detail, red wines should be at room temperature and white wines and sparkling wines should be properly chilled. Red wines should be opened prior to tasting, and any wine should have the opportunity to rest from shipping or handling. Old wines with sediment should be decanted.

During the evaluation itself, these conditions can be changed to reveal different aspects of the wine. For example, some inexpensive white wines have an excellent bouquet (aroma) when they are first opened, but lose it after a few minutes. A restaurateur buying wine for a restaurant in which people linger over a bottle for an evening would consider the durability of the wine's attractiveness an important purchase point.

The taste of wine changes with temperature variation. An acceptable white wine at 40 degrees F. may be undrinkable at 70 degrees F. A young red wine which is unacceptable at "room temperature" may be quite pleasant when slightly chilled. If the purchaser anticipates a temperature variation from normal serving temperatures when the wine is ultimately served, he should duplicate that variation at the tasting.

Glasses

The standard wine glass, a stemmed 8-ounce tulip glass, should be used rather than any specialty glass. The glass must be absolutely clean and well polished. Ideally, it will be of crystal (glass that includes lead compounds in its formulation) and not have the slightly curled edge called a safety rim. A separate glass should be provided for each wine.

Step-by-Step Tasting Procedure

Disciplined, orderly tasting is necessary if the wines are to be judged fairly and accurately. Note taking is almost a necessity when tasting related wines.

The purchaser should adopt a definite regular procedure: examining appearance, bouquet, and taste, in that order.

Appearance

1   Fill the wine glass not less than one quarter nor more than one half full.

2 Pick up the glass by its stem and hold it at eye level, preferably between the taster and a window. Examine the wine.

3 Hold the glass, still at eye level, between the taster and a candle or weak light source. Slowly rotate the glass.

4 Holding the glass by the base, swish the wine in the glass so that it washes up and down the walls of the glass. Observe how it drains back into the glass.

Bouquet

5 Holding the glass by the base, swish it again to expose a large amount of wine to the air to release the bouquet.

6 Hold the glass directly under the nose; ideally, the upper half of the glass should be over the taster's nose. Inhale the bouquet.

7 Warm the wine slightly by cupping the base of the globe in the hands, and repeat step 6.

Taste

8 Take a small amount of wine, perhaps a teaspoonful, into the mouth. Allow it to pass over the tongue and palate (roof, sides, and back of mouth).

9 Purse lips and inhale some air to gather the various elements of the wine bouquet and to drive them into the nasal passages, permitting an appreciation of the wine aroma.

10 Spit out the wine.

What to Look for in Evaluating Wine

Appearance

There are five bench marks for judging the appearance of wine:

1 Color
2 Depth of color or intensity of color

3 Clarity or brilliance
4 Deposit or sediment
5 Viscosity or fluidity

Color Although wines are often described as red, rosé (pink), or white, they vary tremendously within these categories. White wines may range from a nearly colorless watery white to a dark amber, with overtones and reflections of green, yellow, straw yellow, and brown apparent in many white wines. Rosé wines vary from a true rosé, a very light pink, to a rich cherry color. Wines which are described as red may in fact be ruby, garnet, purple, violet, brick red, dark cherry, or orange.

Color is a valuable point of reference in two ways: (1) individual wines have characteristic colors which can be noted for reference; when they are "sick" or adulterated the color will vary; and (2) some objective observations are possible from an examination of a wine's color, once the taster has had some experience in evaluation—that is, has some referent for comparison.

In red wines a genuinely purple color, especially in a wine which is not ordinarily purplish, indicates immaturity. Wine in the cask is purple; in the bottle it develops other colors.

As the wine matures, it loses its purple color and becomes closer to a ruby red. If a bluish color is apparent in a supposedly mature wine, it probably means that the wine has been adulterated.

Older red wines may have a red-brown or even amber-brown coloring, especially apparent at the point where the wine touches the glasses when the glass is tilted. While this coloring is characteristic of mature wines, it should not be present in young wines. Premature browning usually indicates that the wine has been overheated during fermenting or has become oxidized.

Unlike red wines, which gradually lighten in color

with age, white wines become darker. For example, a sweet wine is more yellow when young. After maturing it becomes golden.

A touch of brown in a young wine indicates that it will not keep well. A definite brownish tinge in an older wine indicates that it is mature, most likely over-mature. When a white wine has become oxidized, it takes on the color of Madeira—a definite yellow brown —and is described as "maderized."

Rosés of quality have a definite pink color that departs significantly from the light red of watered-down red wine. A little orange is acceptable, especially in rosé from hot climates, but excess orange color is not. Purple and blue notes in a rosé signal deterioration or improper manufacture.

Depth of Color   Depth of color requires some experience to analyze. There is a definite difference between a ruby-red wine and a deep ruby-red wine, although in each instance the color is only describable as "ruby red." A high color intensity indicates that the grapes used are of high quality, ripe, fully developed, and well nourished, and that the wine was properly processed. A pallid color, although the same color, indicates a poor year or an accelerated processing.

Clarity   When a wine is held up to a candle or a weak light bulb, or placed in a silver saucer-shaped cup with a pebbly bottom, called a "tastevin," the glints of light passing through it show its degree of clarity and highlight and floating or suspended particles.

The wine should be clear, bright, and somewhat shiny. Haze, cloudiness, and dullness are definitely bad signs. The evaluator should not be misled by bits of cork or some floating sediment. Neither reflects on the quality of the wine, merely its handling. Likewise, wines which have just recently been shipped, or subjected to radical changes of temperature, may be momentarily clouded, and this should be considered.

Deposit   Deposit or sediment is more apparent in the bottle than in the glass. As wines age, they may throw off certain compounds, specifically pigments, tannins, and mineral salts, which settle to the bottom of the bottle, either immediately if they are heavy, or after some time if they are "flaky." While sediment is not necessarily a sign of a great wine, it is characteristic of many mature excellent wines, and should not be an immediate cause for rejection.

Viscosity or Fluidity   When the wine is swished in the glass almost to the rim, it may either fall back into the base quickly, or cling to the sides of the glass and fall back in "tears" or "legs." This heavy, transparent film is indicative of richness and is quite prized.

In addition to these factors, sparkling wines might also be judged for the fineness of their bubbles and the longevity of the evanescence.

Bouquet

Each wine has a characteristic bouquet or "nose" which is comprised of two elements: (1) the aroma characteristic of the grapes from which the wine was made; and (2) the perfume, which is the smell acquired during fermentation in the vat, aging in the cask, and maturation in the bottle. In a young wine the aroma is strong; gradually the perfume dominates.

Objective assessment by smell is not directed to the evaluation of a specific bouquet, which the purchaser may or may not like, but to intensity of the bouquet and its cleanliness.

The bouquet of wine can vary in intensity from full or most intense to evasive or least intense. In general, the following terms describe descending intensities:

full, pronounced, delicate, subtle, light, and evasive.

Cleanliness or lack of cleanliness should be immediately apparent. The first impression counts, as the nose quickly becomes fatigued. Any "off smell" should be a cause for rejection: vinegar, rotten eggs, metals, wet rope, cooked cabbage, mold, ink, mustiness, or woodiness.

It is also possible that there may be an unpleasant "cork smell" because the wine's cork has decayed. Although the smell is unforgettable, "corked" or "corky" wines are extremely rare.

Taste

The more objective aspects of taste can be separated from less objective characteristics of wine or its flavor. The taste of wine is essentially limited to its sweetness, acidity, bitterness, harshness and roughness, richness or body, alcohol content, and the persistence of its aftertaste. Particular flavors, for example, a raspberry flavor, like a particular bouquet, characterize individual wines.

There must be sugar in a wine for it to taste sweet. If fermentation has been complete, as is the case in most red wines, the wine will be dry, not sweet at all. White wines, which are more likely to contain some sugar, vary from extremely dry to very sweet. A high alcohol content or high acidity (*see* below) would tend to mask sweetness, and vice versa.

The absence of sugar does not make a wine "acid"; it makes it "dry." Likewise a wine may be both sweet and acid. Acidity, in other words, is a separate dimension of taste, not a degree of sweetness. After sweetness, the most apparent taste characteristic, acidity is most noticeable. Medium acidity gives wine character, while too much acidity can make wine taste sharp, tart, or green or make it undrinkable, and too little can make it appear dull, listless, and flat.

Bitterness is also another dimension of taste, distinct from acidity. By way of definition, quinine is the most common bitter substance and characterizes bar bitters, tonic water, and apéritif drinks. Some wine may have this taste (although it is not due to quinine), and some people may find it pleasant in moderation.

Harshness or hardness is due to the presence of tannin compounds and therefore is more characteristic of the taste of young wines. Tannin is precipitated as a wine ages. In fact, in allowing a wine to age or mature in the bottle, one is really waiting for it to rid itself of the excess tannin that is hiding its qualities.

Three factors contribute to the body of the wine, or how "heavy" it feels in the mouth: the dissolved material in it; the alcoholic content; and the glycerine which gives the wine its unctuousness. On these bases, a wine may appear to be full, flat, and heavy or slight, slender, and light. Depending on the individual wine, body may be an asset or a defect in some people's opinion. Certainly a full-bodied Champagne, for example, would appear unusual.

Aftertaste or finish might be better described as the persistence of characteristic taste and flavor. Quality wines continue to offer the same taste profile as they are tasted, and the taste of the wine remains on the tongue even after the wine has been swallowed. Poorly made wines change taste, literally in the taster's mouth, and disappear the instant they are swallowed.

Knowing What to Expect in a Particular Wine

A quality standard is easily established for certain aspects of a wine's appearance, bouquet, and taste. Nobody likes a muddy wine with a locker-room smell and a hair-tonic taste: it's a *bad* wine. Even if its characteristics are not that dramatic, a wine may be fairly evaluated by anybody, even a first-time wine drinker, in terms of its intensity of flavor, pleasantness of bouquet, astringency of taste, etc. The problem in

evaluating wine is not in judging these aspects and re-
jecting the wines which have little interest, dull appearance, little bouquet, and an unpleasant taste. The
difficulty is in evaluating wines that are acceptable by
those aspects of appearance, bouquet, and taste that
can be made objective. Why is attractive looking,
pleasant smelling, pleasant tasting wine X worth ten
times as much as attractive looking, pleasant smelling,
pleasant tasting wine Y? Wine X has very hard to de-
fine qualities which make it the best of its kind, the
rare wine which is distinguished in a company of good
wines, the masterwork wine which is sublime, not
merely beautiful.

If the purchaser is aware of the qualities of ordinary
and ordinary good wines of its kind, he will recognize a distinguished wine. The purchaser should also
be able to direct his attention toward those qualities
which can distinguish a wine of the particular type
being evaluated. For example, distinguished German
white wine will have a fruity bouquet, the attractive
smell associated with a good ripe fruit, whether it is
peach, plum, apple, or pear. On the other hand, a distinguished mature red Bordeaux will not taste fruity
at all.

The purchaser may also encounter "special" bou-
quets and flavors in particular wines which can be
misleading if he does not expect them. For example,
the Italian red wine Bonarda d'Asti has a sweet aroma
of violets that is likely to surprise the taster pleasantly,
while the excellent French Bordeaux Pétrus can have
a slightly woody taste that will disturb him unneces-
sarily.

In sum, in evaluating wines for purchase on this
basis, the taster should have had a prior experience
with the wine at a tasting or in a restaurant and either
an accurate memory or good notes. He should also
have some information on the particular characteristics
of the wine from having discussed it or read about it.

Wine Description

The more specific and particular characteristics of a wine's bouquet and flavor cannot be accurately described, except in those rare instances when they can be likened to another smell or flavor; for example, that of roses or strawberries. After an accurate description of the wine's objective qualities, even experienced tasters' notes deteriorate. *Typical* is the term most commonly used to identify a hard-to-describe bouquet and flavor. Some descriptive words have a more or less standard referent and are somewhat more helpful in communicating a wine's qualities without drinking the wine.

In addition to those terms already discussed, those which are self-evident, such as "sulphury," and those which defy intelligent definition, although widely used (perhaps for that reason), such as "noble," "breed," "character," and "finesse," the terms listed below frequently occur in wine discussion and literature.

Austere	Refers to the bouquet of young wines which have quality but which at the moment are undeveloped and immature
Balanced	Indicates that all the wine's features complement one another well and together are a harmonious whole
Coarse	Said of a rough, raw-tasting wine that shows no promise of ever becoming smooth; a sign not of immaturity but of lack of quality
Common	Drinkable and pleasant but nothing special
Deep	Indicates that the bouquet and flavor of the wine have numerous overtones; that is, that the flavor or bouquet is complex

Dumb	Said of a wine that is promising but as yet undeveloped; the connotation here is *mute*, not *stupid*
Flat	Lacking interest, insipid, probably because of insufficient acidity
Flinty	An actual taste that refers to the smell of gun flint; a pleasant bite, a clean sharpness
Foxy	An actual taste associated with grapes of the native American vines, perhaps best described (although unfairly) as slightly fetid
Green	Said of wines that are not ripe, in the sense of green fruit
Heady	High in alcoholic content
Light	Means either low alcoholic content or a lack of body
Meaty	Means, along with similar words like *fleshy*, that the wine is rich in suspended and dissolved material and has a very discernible mouth feel
Mellow	Said of wines that are smooth, mature, and ripe and have no astringency
Penetrating	Indicates that the wine's bouquet quickly fills the nasal passages
Piquant	A pleasant acid taste, not sharp but attractively tart, except of course when the wine should not be acid at all
Ordinary	Similar to *common*, but it is less of a pejorative because no disappointment is implied
Robust	Indicates that the wine is full bodied and very strong in its flavor statement but still has quality and no really bad features
Rounded	The same as *balanced* or *well balanced*

Sound	Well-made, free of defects, but not something said of a great wine, which presumably has something more to commend it than the absence of faults
Stalky	Means, with other terms like *twiggy* and *stemmy,* that there is an excess of flavor from skins, stalks, seeds, and stems
Sturdy	Said of a wine that will age well

Guidelines for
the Storage
and the Care
of Wine

Before considering how to store wine, the individual consumer and the restaurateur should address a much more fundamental matter: Why store wine at all beyond immediate needs?

There are two very strong arguments against large-scale long-term storage: (1) most wines are at their best relatively young; improvement after a year in the bottle is the exception, not the rule; and (2) the wine merchant is much better equipped to store and care for wine; only in very few instances can wine be considered a profitable investment.

The purchaser can find himself in a situation where he has considerable sums of money invested in deteriorating wines that he cannot consume or sell, when he might have simply purchased wines on a continuing basis in quantities that reflected his needs.

Very often, on the liquidation of an estate or a restaurant or a hotel operation, expert appraisers discover innumerable bottles many years past their peak. Anyone who buys them is offering 20:1 odds that he will find them drinkable. The original purchaser has lost his investment and whatever return he might have realized by a better-placed investment of the same funds.

The obvious, prudent course for both the consumer and the restaurateur is to transfer the problem and the risks to a merchant or purveyor. Storage by individual consumers and restaurateurs should be limited severely.

There are only three justifications for storage of even as few as five bottles: (1) a definite savings as opposed to a speculative investment, (2) convenience, and (3) "wine collecting," either as a personal hobby or as part of commercial image building.

In certain parts of the country, the restrictive liquor laws make it advantageous, indeed necessary, for both individuals and restaurants to purchase wine in quantity. Otherwise, they would be restricted to the few bottles offered by the state-controlled stores. In these instances, storing wine, provided the proper wines are chosen, can effect a savings.

Convenience is definitely an argument for storing some wine. The individual should have a cellar sufficient to supply sudden fancies and ordinary table use, and the restaurateur should have in his inventory enough wine to assure his customers their choice. On the other hand, only a certain amount of wine can be justified on the basis of convenience. No individual needs cases of Vouvray, and no restaurateur needs cases of Graves.

Wine collecting can be a worthwhile hobby, but the hobbyist must realize that he will be paying for his pastime in bottles he cannot possibly drink before they deteriorate. By the same token, the restaurateur who has chosen to establish a romantic and well-stocked wine cellar for the enjoyment of his guests has to assign some of the cost of the wine he loses to publicity, merchandising, or interior decoration. Often, in these circumstances, the very worst thing possible happens: The connoisseur drinks wines on the edge of undrinkability as the restaurateur with the magnificent cellar pushes bottles which have begun to decline to minimize his losses.

Personal Cellar Lists and Restaurant Wine Menus

The individual consumer, purchasing for personal consumption, and the restaurateur, purchasing for restaurant sales, have almost identical concerns. They both want wines that can be consumed on a daily basis as a routine mealtime beverage, and they both want wines that will satisfy an occasional fancy for something different and exciting. To pursue the parallel, they both need a cellar that emphasizes ready-to-drink, pleasant, moderately priced wines but offers some exotic, more expensive bottles.

It may be that both the consumer and the restaurateur will come to a similar conclusion in regard to the everyday wine: purchase of quality domestic wines in gallons for use in carafes. The wines are good, pleasant, consistent, readily available, and inexpensive. The consumer may choose to drink decent wine with every meal instead of splurging on an occasional grand bottle or playing a vinous Russian roulette with inexpensive imported wines. The restaurateur may decide he can make more money by having more people drink wine with their meals than he can by offering only expensive wines at inflated prices.

The cellars of better bottles can also be very similar; only the total quantity of bottles will differ, not the representation of wines. In fact, the only difference between a modest personal cellar and an extensive one is the number of bottles that would be recommended, not the kinds of wine, and perhaps the emphasis in the modest cellar on types of wine rather than of particular estates.

The following cellar is based on one hundred bottles (100 percent) so that a proportional representation of wine types and imported and domestic wines is apparent. Obviously, an individual may want to scale down his personal cellar, while a restaurateur may well convert bottles into cases, depending on his volume of business.

TABLE 4.1. REPRESENTATIVE WINE CELLAR

WINE CLASSIFICATION		NUMBER OF BOTTLES (%)
		Total
Red wines	49%	
White wines	45%	
Rosé wines	6%	
		100%
Still wines	94%	
Sparkling wines	6%	
		100%

WINE CLASSIFICATION		NUMBER OF BOTTLES (%)
Imported		Total
French	48%	
Non-French	27%	
		75%
Domestic		
California	20%	
New York	5%	
		25%
		100%

WINE CLASSIFICATION		NUMBER OF BOTTLES
Red wines		Total
French		
Bordeaux		
Appellation		
Contrôlée	6	
Classed		
Châteaux	8	
		14

Burgundy
    Beaujolais   2
    Gevrey-
      Chambertin   2
    Nuits Saint-
      George   1
    Volnay   1
    Pommard   1
    Vosne-
      Romanée   2
    Château-
      neuf-du-
      Pape   1
    Côte-Rôtie   1
    Hermitage   1
    V.D.Q.S.   <u>2</u>

                                   14

Italian
    Barolo   2
    Chianti   2
    Barbaresco   1
    Grignolino   1
    Barbera   1
    Valpolicella   <u>1</u>

                                   8

Other imported
    vintage Port
      (Portugal)   1
    Sherry
      (Spain)   <u>1</u>

                                 2

Domestic
    California
      varietals   8
    California
      Sherry   1
    New York
      varietal   1
    California
      sparkling
      Burgundy   <u>1</u>

                                 11

Rosé

California	2	
New York	1	
Tavel (France)	1	
Anjou (France)	1	
Provence (France)	1	
		6

White Wines

French
Bordeaux

Appellation Contrôlée	2	
Classed Châteaux	2	
		4

Burgundy

Chablis	2	
Pouilly-Fuissé	1	
Montrachet	1	
Meursault	1	
		5

Other

Alsace	2	
Muscadet	1	
Vouvray	1	
Champagne	2	
V.D.Q.S.	2	
		8

Italian

Capri	1	
Soave	1	
Montefiascone	1	
Frascati	1	
Verdicchio	1	
Chianti	1	
Orvieto	1	
Asti Spumanti	1	
		8

German		
Rhine	2	
Rheinhessen	1	
Moselle	3	
Nahe	1	
Franconia	1	
Palatinate	1	
	—	
		9
Domestic		
California varietal	7	
California Champagne	1	
New York varietal	2	
New York Champagne	1	
	—	
		11
		100

The Wine "Cellar"

Traditionally cellars were used for wine storage because they provided desirable temperature and humidity. With modern air conditioning, the wine "cellar" may be located anywhere and may be any size from the specially manufactured closetlike cellars to vast commercial warehouses.

Physical Requirements for the Storage of Wine

Any area for the storage of wine should be:

1 Not less than 48 degrees F or more than 64 degrees F at any time
2 Vibration-free
3 Sheltered from the direct rays of the sun
4 Free of substances that emit strong odors
5 Spotlessly clean
6 Relatively dry, but not arid
7 Ventilated

The wines should be stored on racks or in bins off the floor of the cellar. Commercial racks are available, starting with modules that accommodate three bottles. Or bins may be constructed so that the wines may be stored at a slight slant to keep the bottom of the corks moistened. Ideally, the center of the top of the cork should be just slightly higher than the center of the bottle's bottom, so that the air bubble is in the center of the bottle.

Handling Wine Bottles

Highly processed wines, such as those sold in gallon containers, can be shipped and moved without any ill effect. Other wines are more vulnerable and can develop a temporary cloudiness after traveling. Wines with sediment normally have the sediment shaken throughout the bottle during transit. These wines must be rested before they are used.

Wines with sediment always must be handled gently. Ideally, the wine will remain undisturbed in an out-of-the-way place in the wine cellar until it is used.

Decanting Wines

Wines that have developed a sediment should be decanted, or poured from the original bottle into a serving vessel, before they are served. Although the wine may be poured directly from the bottle into wine glasses, there is necessarily more waste, and it is likely that some sediment will get into the glasses. In addition to separating the wine from its sediment, decanting also accelerates the oxidation of the wine; sometimes wines are decanted for this reason alone. Most of the time, only mature quality red wines must be decanted; but some varietals develop a sediment, and it is possible to find one in a heavy white wine.

Figure 4.1. A decanting basket is often used to hold a bottle of wine to be decanted.

To decant a wine, a spotlessly clean decanter, preferably of clear glass or crystal; a clean cloth; a candle or light source; and a funnel, preferably of silver, are needed. A decanting cradle or basket may also be used if difficulty in holding the bottle is anticipated.

1 Gently take the wine from the rack or bin.
2 Remove the seal around the cork.
3 Clean the top of the bottle.
4 Drive the corkscrew deep into the center of the cork, without shaking the bottle or allowing the corkscrew to touch the sides of the bottle.
5 Remove the cork as gently as possible, using a long even pull.
6 Check to see that the wine is healthy: it is pointless to decant a spoiled wine.
7 Clean the inside of the neck of the bottle with the cloth.
8 Place the funnel in the decanter.
9 Place the bottle in the cradle or basket if one is being used.
10 Place the candle so that when the right elbow is rested on the table, holding the bottle, the candle illuminates the neck of the bottle.
11 Pour the wine from the original bottle into the funnel, taking care to let it spread down the side of the decanter, rather than pouring it into the bottom.

12 Pour the wine steadily, without stopping.
13 Stop pouring when a cloud of sediment appears
    in the neck of the bottle.
14 The wine remaining in the bottle may be filtered
    and used for cooking. A filter should *not* be used
    for the wine being decanted for drinking, as is
    sometimes recommended, for there is every likeli-
    hood of fatiguing a delicate wine unnecessarily.

Recordkeeping

There is little use in keeping wines unless they are
carefully followed as they mature. The individual consumer may use an ornate cellarbook, while the restaurateur uses less romantic but more businesslike bin
cards, but the basic information each requires is the
same:

1 When the wine was purchased
2 How much was paid
3 The merchant's name
4 Initial evaluation if the wine was tasted, or the
   catalog description, or a clipping of the article
   that prompted its purchase
5 An appropriate tasting note (if possible) for each
   bottle as it is used
6 Updated information on the wine, especially price
   changes
7 A recommendation for future purchases

Serving Wine

The object of serving wine properly is to enhance the drinker's pleasure. While details of wine service can be overemphasized and the ritual can detract from the wine, a too-casual service will not present the wine well. Having purchased the wine, and perhaps having nurtured it, it would be unfortunate to miss the opportunity to enjoy it fully.

Preparing Wine for Service

Allowing Wines to "Breathe"

Wine in the bottle is biologically dead but chemically alive. It reacts strongly to the presence of oxygen, which is why so much importance is attached to the soundness of the cork during maturation.

When a wine is to be drunk, additional oxygen chemically feeds the flavor and the bouquet. The wine loses its "storage" taste and smell.

There are no absolute rules for determining how long a wine should be allowed to stand opened before being served. Among the most important aspects of the sommelier's stewardship is a bottle-by-bottle decision on this matter. Experience with the particular wine is undoubtedly the best guideline.

Some general observations are possible. Wines with discernible carbonation are served immediately. White wines and very young wines generally profit by a half hour. Rosés, with very rare exceptions, do not. A mature red wine up to 8 years old realizes its full potential at about 2½ hours. On the other hand, very mature wines (25 years old, for example) may be too delicate to be "traumatized" by an onrush of oxygen. Often they must be served immediately, or their final greatness, their swan song bouquet and flavor, wanes. Between 8 and 25 years, a proportionate breathing space is indicated. It is better to underexpose than to overexpose a wine.

Serving Temperature of Wine

Ultimately, the temperature at which a wine is served is a matter of taste. Different people appreciate different aspects of a wine's quality as they are revealed at different temperatures. However, the majority of people—amateurs and professionals alike—agree on some general guidelines. The way the wine reacts to various temperatures determines the basic rules.

The lowest acceptable temperature appears to be about 36 degrees F for very dry sparkling wines; the top limit for red wines is about 72 degrees F. Below 36 degrees F the wine risks having most of its character frozen. Above 72 degrees F undesirable flavor elements dominate.

Most white wines are chilled to about 45 degrees F, but high-alcohol or very sweet wines can be cooled to 42 degrees F. It should be remembered that once the wine is poured, its temperature climbs rapidly and overchilling is quickly rectified.

Most red wines are best savored at 65 degrees F. Red wines without much body or with unpleasant roughness profit by chilling.

Ideally, wine is chilled (or warmed) in a room or area of the proper temperature. It can also be chilled satisfactorily in a refrigerator. A freezer compartment may cause it to "break," or precipitate tartaric acid crystals, by chilling it too quickly. Ten minutes in a bucket filled with crushed ice will chill a bottle, 20 minutes will really make it cold, and 45 minutes will make it ice cold. The bottle may be shifted around in the bucket or even inverted so that the wine in the neck is chilled as well.

Opening Wine Bottles

Choice of a Corkscrew

Somebody who has a cellar full of wine or who consumes a bottle a night certainly can afford several

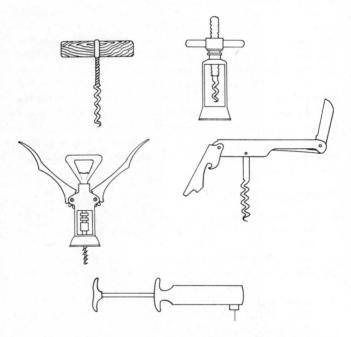

Figure 5.1. There are various types of corkscrews available for use in opening bottles of wine. *Top:* Traditional; double helix. *Center:* Double-handled lever; professional waiter combination. *Bottom:* Compressed air extractor.

corkscrews, each for a particular kind of cork. If it is well designed, the traditional corkscrew, a wormlike screw fitted into a double screw of wood or metal, or a professional waiter combination penknife and lever works well for most corks. The screw part should be long enough to extend through the cork. Since some wines have long corks, a length of at least 2½ inches is needed. The open, perfectly round wire helix, with an off-center point, a hollow core of about ⅛ inch, and an outside diameter of ⅜ inch, and 6 complete spirals works best.

Old corks are easy to remove using a tweezerlike cork extractor that does not penetrate the cork but breaks its seal on the side of the bottle. The needle extractor which injects gas or compressed air under the cork also works well for old corks.

Very young or unseasoned corks require some strength to remove. Double helix corkscrews, which facilitate a cork-wrenching twist, are useful. A good worm screw in a double-handled lever device, a professional wine waiter's lever penknife, and a screw-action or a screw and bell device. also facilitate removal.

Opening Still Wines

1   Cut the tinfoil or plastic "capsule" at the lip of the wine bottle. The little disc may be removed or left on a hinge.

2   Wipe the bottle's neck and lip with a clean cloth.

3   Insert the corkscrew directly into the center of the cork. It must be centered.

4   Grasping the corkscrew in the right hand and the bottle in the left, turn the corkscrew into the cork up to the shank.

5   Either pull the cork directly but not all the way, or start it with a twist and edge it toward the top of the bottle.

6   Unscrew the corkscrew.
7   Using the fingers and thumb of the right hand, still grasping the bottle in the left hand, lever the cork from the bottle. There should be no pop or rush of air into the bottle. Work slowly; avoid dripping and spattering.
8   Using the corner of a clean cloth, clean the bottle opening to remove any grime or fragments of cork.

Opening Sparkling Wines

Champagne and other sparkling wines are not sealed with ordinary corks, because the wine is carbonated and under pressure. The bottle is closed with a special high-quality mushroom-shaped cork which protrudes and is in turn covered by a twisted wire, and then with metal foil.

1   Make sure the sparkling wine is chilled before attempting to open it.
2   Take the wine from a wine bucket or refrigerator using a cloth. Do not touch the bottle with the bare hands, as a sudden change of temperature can break the bottle. Wrap the cloth around the bottle.
3   Twist the little wire loop that protrudes from the tinfoil until the wire loosens or the loop breaks off.
4   Remove the wire. The foil will come off with the wire.
5   Keep the thumb of the right hand on the top of the cork.
6   Hold the bottle at a 45-degree angle (halfway between straight up and parallel to the floor).
7   Point the bottle away from everyone.
8   Holding the bottle with the left hand, twist the bottle to loosen the cork.

9   Ease the pressure of the thumb *slightly*. The pressure inside the bottle should slowly force the cork from the bottle. It should slide out with no pop or geyser.

10 Keep the bottle in an inclined position for 5 seconds to equalize the pressure inside the bottle with the atmospheric pressure.

If the mushroom cap of the cork should break off, the bottle must be opened with a regular corkscrew. Unfortunately, this is a difficult procedure, as Champagne corks are highly compressed, excellent quality cork, and it is likely that the corkscrew will break before the bottle is opened.

Opening Old Port

Ports and other wines that are destined for a long life are sealed with extra-long corks that fill the neck of the bottle and mushroom slightly when they enter its shoulders. If the bottle has been recorked within the last 15 or 20 years there should be little problem in removing it. Long-lived bottles are periodically recorked because the wine outlives the cork. If the cork is very old, it may be impossible to remove, even using a tweezer-type extractor, or the cork may crumble into the bottle.

In this instance the best course is to knock the neck off the bottle. Hobby stores sell a "glass saw" for making artifacts from bottles, which works well to score the bottle so that a sharp rap with a heavy knife breaks the neck cleanly. A conventional glass cutter also works, or the bottle may be scored, with less consistent success, with a heavy knife. When Port was in vogue in the old homes of England, special tongs were heated and applied to the bottle's neck to cause the glass to snap.

Glassware

Type of Glass

The numerous specialty glasses for wine should be evaluated against the ideal glass. The ideal glass is thin clear crystal without flaws. It has a sturdy base and comfortable stem. The bowl is slightly tulip-shaped with an opening that will comfortably admit a man's nose. The glass will hold eight ounces filled to a brim unmarred by a safety rim.

Colored, etched, or textured glasses distort a wine's appearance. Clumsy glasses—for example, little bowls on high stems—make it difficult to examine. Thick glasses give it a different "mouth-feel." Too small glasses do not concentrate the bouquet, and too big glasses risk causing the delicate bouquet of the old wines usually served in this kind of glass to disintegrate by being overexposed.

Cleanliness of Glassware

Any smell or taste adhering to glassware will be communicated to the wine and amplified by it. Often specialty glassware is stored in closed cupboards, where it acquires a musty odor. Many modern detergent compounds leave a slight scent or a chemical residue that prevents streaking which can be communicated to the wine. It is best to redip washed wine glasses in hot water and polish them with clean cloths to ensure perfect cleanliness.

Pouring Wine

1   Place the right hand over the bottle with the thumb on one side and the fingers around the other. Never grip a bottle by the neck or the punt (well in the bottom of the bottle).

2   Hold the right index finger on the shoulder of the bottle, not on its neck.

3   Place the lip of the bottle just over the edge of the glass.

4   Using the wrist, tip the bottle slowly downward until the wine begins to flow.

5   When the glass is sufficiently full, pivot the wrist to move the hand upward. Fill glass half full for red wine and three-fourths full for white.

6   To fill glasses with sparkling wine, repeat step five. The wine is poured once, it froths, and when the froth has settled it is poured again.

7   As the bottle leaves the downward position, give it a gentle quarter twist to avoid dripping wine.

8   Touch the lip of the bottle with a clean cloth after each pouring to prevent dripping.

Formal or Restaurant Wine Service

Beyond the technical procedures of preparing wine for service, opening the bottles, and pouring the wine, there is a technique for wine service for situations in which a domestic or a waiter is serving, or the host wishes to be quite formal.

Setting the Glasses

Glasses are set above the right side of the place setting. If one glass is used, the point of the main course knife should be in line with the stem of the glass. Other glasses are ranged to the right in a straight line from this glass. The order may be in order of service, starting at the extreme right; or the glasses may be arranged from the right, smallest to largest. When three glasses are set, the glasses can be arranged in a triangle: one glass above the knife, one glass to the right of it, and one glass below the second glass.

Presenting Bottles of Wine

Before the bottle of wine is poured, the waiter in a restaurant presents it to the guest. A domestic servant would present it to the head of the household. The host is assured by seeing the bottle that he is getting the wine he ordered—there has been no substitution.

1   Approach the customer or the host from his right side.
2   Holding the neck of the bottle in the left hand, cradle the bottle in the right palm using a cloth.
3   Tilt the bottle gently so that the customer or host can easily read the label.
4   Announce the name of the wine and the vintage, if any; for example, "The Pétrus 1959, sir."
5   Do not shake the wine while handling it.

In a restaurant, the presentation would necessarily precede decanting in a pantry area. In a home there is no presentation, as the wine is decanted before the meal. The domestic may indicate, usually with an audible whisper to the host, the name and vintage of the wine before he serves it.

Etiquette of Service

At a formal dinner or in a restaurant the host is served first so that he may judge the wine and accept it or reject it. He may be served, or may serve himself, a full glass after this first taste so that any cork fragments in the bottle will be poured into his glass. After he has been served or given the wine to taste, his guests are served. Practices vary, but most often the ladies are served first, starting with the lady on the host's right side.

When a second wine is offered, or even a second bottle of the same wine, the glasses are changed.

Wine and the Menu

Wine may be enjoyed any time of the day in any circumstance. Americans are discovering a number of traditional European pleasures: a glass of wine instead of midmorning or afternoon coffee; wine "coolers" instead of sweet carbonated sodas; wine as a cocktail; wine as an evening refreshment; and wine as a nightcap.

More important, they are discovering that wine is the perfect ordinary accompaniment to meals, not just a special-occasion treat. Both restaurateurs and individual consumers must ask themselves which wines go with which foods.

Old Rules, New Rules, and No Rules

Enough research will probably turn up an "expert" with a precise recommendation (château and vintage) for the "right" wine to have with cornflakes. So much has been written about wine by people so sure of their own tastes that it is possible to become a devoted acolyte in a wine religion with a complete dogma and catechism. On the other hand, even the most superficial investigation will produce "experts" who delight in heresy for itself. The prospect of sacrificing a great bottle to a chocolate pudding fascinates them.

It is a mistake to dismiss tradition, the codified experience of millions of other wine drinkers. There is a great deal of common sense among the snobbery. It is also a mistake to revere it. Tastes differ. For example, Europeans like wines warmer than do Americans; Germans enjoy their white wines at as much as 10 degrees warmer. Tastes change. Heavy Port is "out," but it still dominates much of traditional English wine and gastronomic literature.

The Color Question

The traditional rule, red wine with red meat, white wine with white meat, is so pockmarked by exceptions that it cannot be applied as such. Yet there is still some merit in it. Essentially, the individual wine and the individual dish must be considered.

There is no doubt that white wines generally suit fish dishes better than red wines, but the converse is often demonstrably not true: white wines frequently suit red meats, except when they have been prepared with a red wine sauce.

Red wines taste less pleasant when the fish dish is very "fishy," with a taste of the sea, or if it has a very metallic alkaline taste, especially when the red wine itself is rough, full of unmatured tannins. On the other hand, quality reds seem to suit the fattier fishes like salmon. A convenient resolution of the problem can often be found in traditional classic cookbooks: If there are dishes for a fish using red wine, then red wine is a suitable accompaniment.

Another rule, that rosé wine can be drunk with everything, is also vulnerable. A very light rosé is really a white wine, while a very dark rosé resembles a light red. Even when the rosé is truly pink, it may be dry or sweet, full-bodied or light, or have any number of other qualities which will make it unsuitable for certain dishes.

Wine Games

A great deal of the disenchantment with traditional wine rules is due to the impossibility of playing the wine games that European (mostly English) connoisseurs developed for their own amusement. In a time and place when wines were available and inexpensive, it was possible to decide to drink specific wines with specific foods on all sorts of arbitrary bases. The geographical game was very popular, and at least two of its rules seem to have become part of traditional ritual: (1) Drink national wines with national dishes, and (2) drink regional wines with food produced in the same region.

Many people enjoy paella, a Spanish dish of rice, vegetables, saffron, and other seasonings garnished with chicken, seafood, and sausage. Unfortunately, many of the Spanish wines imported into the United States are very inexpensive and, even at low prices, are a poor value. It is basically unfair to the dish to serve it with an inadequate Spanish wine just because the wine is Spanish.

Drinking regional wines with regional foods has a certain romantic appeal. Imagine eating a local cheese with a glass of local wine while the goat from whose milk the cheese was made munches on the wine-producing grape vine. On the spot the romance may be sufficient compensation for bad cheese or bad wine, but several thousand miles away practicality displaces romance. Some regions that produce excellent food products like cheese or fruit produce very bad wine, if they produce any wine at all. Normandy, in France, for example, produces Brie, Camembert, and other excellent cheeses, cider, and perry. No one would seriously contend that French Burgundy and Bordeaux wines could be displaced by apple juice as a suitable drink for cheese. By the same token, fine wine is produced from grapes which grow in very inhospitable places on unfertile soils.

Water and Wine

Traditional wine connoisseurs are absolutely repelled at the idea of watering wine or in any way adulterating it. Without doubt, adding water fundamentally changes a wine. The drinker must really ask himself why the particular bottle was purchased: Will adulteration with water, carbonated water, fruit juice, or a soda drink diminish or enhance the wine's "purchase points"? If a classed Bordeaux château wine was purchased at a cost considerably above a quality Bordeaux Appellation Contrôlée, dilution will diminish the unique qualities of the wine. The price premium was wasted. On the other hand, if a nice white wine was purchased because it promised to be refreshing, there is every argument for enhancing its refreshing qualities by adding soda and fruit.

The same logic can apply to wines used to accompany ordinary meals. It may be more satisfying to drink great draughts of beverage with a spicy spaghetti dish than to sip decorously at a glass of wine. In this circumstance, conversion of the wine into a wine drink or a wine and water mixture would seem reasonable.

Pouring wine over ice cubes or cracked ice is equally abhorrent to the traditionalist whose rules for wine drinking were developed in chilly, drafty European houses. Many Americans live in hot places, and others keep their homes very warm. Americans basically like cold beverages, beer, and mixed drinks as well as wine. As long as the effects of dilution and chilling are understood, the practice is acceptable.

Basics of Matching Food and Wine

It is important to know the traditional rules, with elements of common sense, even if they will be ignored because of some transcendent personal taste.

1 When several wines are served during a meal, if the full value of the wines is to be appreciated, they must be ordered so that the palate is not prejudiced by the first wines drunk:

    a Dry before sweet

      b   White before red, unless the serving order violates the dry-before-sweet rule
      c   Young before old
      d   Light before full bodied, unless the serving order violates the dry-before-sweet rule
      e   Modest before great
      f   Table wines before fortified wines

2   If a Champagne is used as a table wine, its service should be continued throughout the meal.

3   Very sweet wines are used for dessert courses.

4   Dishes that contain vinegar—or foods that contain it—do not go well with wine: pickles, mustard, ketchup, salad dressing, etc.

5   Madeira or sherry is preferred with soup, unless the soup contains wine, in which case no wine is served.

6   A few good wines are more enjoyable than a confusing variety.

7   Delicate wines should be served with delicate dishes.

8   Robust foods need robust wines to "stand up" to them.

9   Sweet wines should be served with sweet fruits; no wine with citrus fruits.

10   No wine should be served with eggs, except for omelets, which can take medium-quality wines.

Guidelines for Personal Matches of Wine and Food

The individual consumer or restaurateur can establish a number of practical principles for himself which will guide him in matching wine and foods on the basis of his own taste.

1   The wine and the dish should be of about the same flavor order; for example, simple and direct, like pizza with a California mountain red; or a complex but subtle dish like Pike Quenelles in Nantua Sauce with a Montrachet.

TABLE 6.1 SOME SPECIFIC (AND SAFE) SUGGESTIONS

Food	Wine
Beef	Full-bodied reds*
Cake	Cold, sweet white wines
Cheese	
Gruyère (Swiss)	Dry white
Edam or Gouda	Full-bodied red
Semisoft Port Salut	All colors, dry and fruity
Blue	Fortified
Soft	Light reds
Fresh	Crisp whites, rosés
Processed	All colors, dry
Goat and sheep	Tart whites
Chicken	
Hot	Red wines*
Cold	Semidry whites
Coffee	Vintage Port
Desserts in general	Sweet whites, Champagne
Eggs in general	No wine
Omelets	Light reds
Fish	Dry whites and rosés*
Foie Gras	
Preserved	Fortified
Fresh	Dry reds
Fruit	
Apples	Red wines
Citrus fruit	No wine
Strawberries	Port
Other fruit	Sweet whites
Game	Full-bodied red*
Ham	Light white*
Hors d'ouevre preparation	No wine
Ice cream	No wine
Salad	No wine

Food	Wine
Lamb	Light red
Poultry	Light red*
Shellfish	
Raw	Dry white
Cooked	White*
Smoked foods	Dry white, dry fortified
Soup	Dry fortified
Made with wine	No wine
Veal	Light reds and whites
Vegetables	Semidry whites, rosés
Carrots	Red
Spinach and similar greens	Dry whites

* Choice should depend on preparation.

2   The wine should either harmonize with the food and complement it, or contrast with the food and thereby reveal it. For example, a dry white wine harmonizes with seafood, and a sweet white wine contrasts with curry.

3   Avoid serving wines with foods that have qualities which if found in the wine would fault it. Vinegary foods and wine are the best example; a taste of vinegar in a wine is a great defect. There are others: Eggs do not go well with wine because of their basic sulphury taste; the blue cheeses go better with fortified wines than with table wines because fortified wines have too much alcohol to support mold.

4   Consider the preparation, not just the main ingredient. A wine served with barbecued chicken is not being served with roasted chicken. The wine has to stand up to ketchup, garlic, lemon juice, pepper, etc.

5   Consider the weather, the mood of the party, and the occasion. For example, a great full-bodied wine

is not right on a hot, humid day, no matter what the menu. Likewise, fortified wines in close, heated, crowded dining rooms make the diner feel uncomfortable.

6   A good dish merits a good wine, even if it is the wrong wine on other bases. In other words, it is better to serve a quality red wine with a fish than to serve an indifferent white wine just because it is white.

Wines of
France

France produces tremendous quantities of wine, imports tremendous quantities of wine, and consumes tremendous quantities of wine. Few of these millions of gallons have any interest at all for the American restaurateur or consumer. Most of the wine produced and exported is the least expensive beverage wine imaginable, blended and bottled by large concerns to be sold for 20 cents a quart, or less if the customer brings his own bottle.

About 10 percent of the wine produced is Appellation Contrôlée, entitled to an official guarantee of origin and quality; of these a much smaller percentage is likely to have real merit, and a still smaller number has the quality of appeal to justify its exportation. For example, the French département (state) where Bordeaux is located, the Gironde, which ranks fourth in total gallonage production but first in production of Appellation Contrôlée wines (75 percent), has over 50,000 vineyard proprietors, and only two thousand of them are worthwhile. Fewer than two hundred of these have given Bordeaux wines world renown. The purchaser might be aware that if a wine is French (or Bordeaux, Burgundy, Côtes-du-Rhône, etc.) it might be great, but its being French is not necessarily a guarantee that it is good.

Most French wines are classified, named, controlled, and labeled on the basis of a very precise geographical organization of the four million acres of vineyards. In some respects, this organization follows the political divisions of the country. Control and quality standards increase as smaller and smaller areas are addressed. For example, a very ordinary wine from over 250,000 acres of vineyards in Gironde can be called a Bordeaux, but only a wine of definite quality standards from a specific 110 acres can be called a Château Latour. It is produced in the Pauillac commune of the Haut-Médoc area of the Médoc region in the *département* of Gironde, France.

Regional names may or may not be Appellation Contrôlée names themselves. Bordeaux is, but Loire is not. This means that if a wine is called Bordeaux on the label it is an Appellation Contrôlée wine. A wine from the Loire will either be called by an Appellation Contrôlée name referring to a smaller area within the Loire: for example, Anjou Appellation Contrôlée; the name of a smaller region designated V.D.Q.S. (Vins Délimités de Qualité Supérieure) a geographical classification system of wines which are less notable than the Appellation Contrôlée; or any name whatsoever so long as it is not fraudulent and does not infringe on the geographical classifications.

Bordeaux

The Bordeaux region produces wines which are among the best in the world. As a producing area, Bordeaux is also unrivaled for the variety of its wines. Three distinct types are produced: (1) the Bordeaux red wines (clarets), (2) the white wines like those of Graves, and (3) the sweet white wines like those of Sauternes. In each of these categories, the best Bordeaux wine equals or exceeds the best wine of regions devoted exclusively to the production of a single type.

The Bordeaux region is divided into eight producing districts, five major and three minor: Médoc, Graves, Sauternes, Saint-Émilion, Pomerol, Côtes, Entre-deux-Mers, and *palus*. Each of these is divided into further subdivisions, or parishes, which contain individual vineyards. The great wines of Bordeaux take their names from vineyard names: Château Margaux, Château Latour, Château Haut-Brion, etc.

The leading châteaux of four districts, Médoc (1855), Sauternes (1855), Graves (1953), and Saint-Émilion (1955), have been classified on the basis of quality. Although there is certainly injustice, and some obsolescence, in these lists, they are widely and justifiably approved. The restaurateur and the individual consumer should not overconclude from this ranking. These lists include only the absolutely greatest Bordeaux wines, not all of them: there remain excellent châteaux classified as Crus Exceptionnels, Crus Bourgeois Supérieurs, and Crus Bourgeois, all below the fifth growth wines (Cinquièmes Crus). There are also excellent châteaux (some the equal of the classed growths) which have not been classified and fine Appellation Contrôlée wines bearing parish names. Within the lists, the ranking is only relative. For example, the difference between the wines is very, very small in the Médoc list, which ranked the 15 best red Bordeaux, although the first growths command higher prices than the second growths, and within growths the higher ranking wines (the first wine of the second growth) are more expensive.

TABLE 7.1. THE 1855 CLASSIFICATION OF MEDOC RED WINES

CHATEAUX	COMMUNE
First Growths	
Lafite	Pauillac
Latour	Pauillac
Margaux	Margaux
Haut-Brion	Pessac (Graves)

Second Growths

Mouton-Rothschild	Pauillac
Lascombes	Margaux
Rausan-Ségla	Margaux
Rausan-Gassies	Margaux
Léoville-Lascases	Saint-Julien
Léoville-Poyferré	Saint-Julien
Léoville-Barton	Saint-Julien
Durfort-Vivens	Margaux
Gruaud Larose	Saint-Julien
Brane-Cantenac	Cantenac-Margaux
Pichon-Longueville	Pauillac
Pichon-Longueville (Comtesse de Lalande)	Pauillac
Ducru-Beaucaillou	Saint-Julien
Cos d'Estournel	Saint-Estèphe
Montrose	Saint-Estèphe

Third Growths

Giscours	Labarde-Margaux
Kirwan	Cantenac-Margaux
d'Issan	Cantenac-Margaux
Lagrange	Saint-Julien
Langoa	Saint-Julien
Malescot-Saint-Exupéry	Margaux
Cantenac-Brown	Cantenac-Margaux
Palmer	Cantenac-Margaux
La Lagune	Ludon
Desmirail	Margaux
Calon-Ségur	Saint-Estèphe
Ferrière	Margaux
Marquis-d'Alesme-Becker	Margaux
Boyd-Cantenac	Margaux

Fourth Growths

Le Prieuré-Lichine	Cantenac-Margaux
Saint Pierre	Saint-Julien
Branaire-Duluc	Saint-Julien
Talbot	Saint-Julien
Duhart-Milon	Pauillac
Pouget	Cantenac-Margaux

La Tour-Carnet	Saint-Laurent
Lafon-Rochet	Saint-Estèphe
Beychevelle	Saint-Julien
Marquis-de-Terme	Margaux

Fifth Growths

Pontet Canet	Pauillac
Batailley	Pauillac
Grand-Puy-Lacoste	Pauillac
Grand-Puy Ducasse	Pauillac
Haut-Batailley	Pauillac
Lynch-Bages	Pauillac
Lynch-Moussas	Pauillac
Dauzac	Labarde-Margaux
Mouton-Baron-Philippe (formerly Chateau Mouton-d'Armailhacq)	Pauillac
Le Tertre	Arsac-Margaux
Haut-Bages-Libéral	Pauillac
Pédesclaux	Pauillac
Belgrave	Saint-Laurent
Camensac	Saint-Laurent
Cos Labory	Saint-Estèphe
Clerc-Milon-Mondon	Pauillac
Croizet Bages	Pauillac
Cantermerle	Macau

Exceptional Growths

Villegeorge	Avensan
Angludet	Cantenac-Margaux
Chasse-Spleen	Moulis
Poujeaux-Thiel	Moulis
La Couronne	Pauillac
Moulin-Riche	Saint-Julien
Bel-Air-Marquis d'Aligre	Soussans-Margaux

TABLE 7.2. THE 1855 CLASSIFICATION OF SAUTERNES WHITE WINES

CHATEAU	COMMUNE
First Great Growth	
d'Yquem	Sauternes

First Growths

Guiraud	Sauternes
La Tour-Blanche	Bommes
Lafaurie-Peyraguey	Bommes
Haut-Peyraguey	Bommes
Rayne-Vigneau	Bommes
Rabaud-Promis	Bommes
Sigalas-Rabaud	Bommes
Coutet	Barsac
Climens	Barsac
Suduiraut	Preignac
Rieussec	Fargues

Second Growths

d'Arche	Sauternes
Filhot	Sauternes
Lamothe	Sauternes
Myrat	Barsac
Doisy-Védrines	Barsac
Doisy-Daëne	Barsac
Suau	Barsac
Broustet	Barsac
Caillou	Barsac
Nairac	Barsac
de Malle	Preignac
Romer	Fargues

TABLE 7.3. THE 1953 CLASSIFICATION OF GRAVES RED AND WHITE WINES

CHATEAU	COMMUNE
Classed Red Wines	
Haut-Brion	Pessac
Bouscaut	Cadaujac
Carbonnieux	Léognan
Domaine (not Ch.) de Chevalier	Léognan
Fieuzal	Léognan
Haut-Bailly	Léognan
La Mission-Haut Brion	Pessac
La Tour Haut-Brion	Talence

La Tour-Martillac	Martillac
Malartic-Lagravière	Léognan
Olivier	Léognan
Pape-Clément	Pessac
Smith-Haut-Lafite	Martillac

Classed White Wines

Bouscaut	Cadaujac
Carbonnieux	Léognan
Domaine (not Ch.) de Chevalier	Léognan
Couhins	Villenave d'Ornon
La Tour-Martillac*	Martillac
Laville-Haut-Brion	Talence
Malartic-Lagravière*	Léognan
Olivier	Léognan

*added in 1959.

1955 Classification of Saint-Emilion Wines

There is no importance (distinguishing characteristics) attached to the Communes of Saint-Émilion wines. Since the châteaux on this list are protected by the A.O.C. laws, they have the weight of an Appellation Contrôlée, while those of Médoc above do not. Names are prefaced by Château unless otherwise indicated.

First Great Growths

Ausone	Canon
Cheval Blanc	Figeac
Beauséjour-Duffau-Lagorrosse	Fourtet
	la Gaffelière-Naudes
Beauséjour-Fagouet	Magdelaine
Belair	Pavie
	Trottevieille

Great Growths

L'Arrosée	La Cluzière
Balestard-la-Tonnelle	La Couspaude
Bellevue	La Dominique

Bergat
Cadet-Bon
Cadet-Piola
Canon-la-Gaffelière
Cap de Mourlin
Chapelle-Madeleine
Chatelet
Chauvin
Clos des Jacobins
Clos de Madeleine
Clos Saint-Martin
Corbin
Corbin-Michotte
Coutet
Croque-Michotte
Curé-Bon
Fonplégade
Fonroque
Franc-Mayne
Grand-Barrail-Lamarzelle-
  Figeac
Grand-Corbin
Grand-Mayne
les Grandes Murailles
Grant Pontet
Gaudet-Saint-Julien
Jeane Fauré
La Carte
La Clotte

La Marzelle
l'Angélus
Larcis-Ducasse
Larmande
Laroze
Lasserre
La Tour-Figeac
La Tour du-Pin-Fingeac
Le Couvent
Le Prieuré
Mauvezin
Moulin-du-Cadet
Pavie Decesse
Pavie-Macquin
Pavillon-Cadet
Petit-Faurie-de-
  Souchard
Petit-Faurie-de-Soutard
Ripeau
Saint-Georges-Côte-
  Pavie
Sansonnet
Soutard
Tertre-Daugay
Trimoulet
Trois-Moulins
Troplong-Mondot
Villemaurine
Yon Figeac

Major Appellations Contrôlées from Bordeaux in Addition to Bordeaux A.O.C.

White

Graves
Cérons
Sauternes
Barsac

Sainte-Croix-du-Mont
Loupiac
Sainte-Foy-Bordeaux
Graves de Vayres

Entre-deux-Mers
Premières Côtes de
   Bordeaux

Côtes de Bordeaux
   Saint-Macaire

Red

Médoc
Haut-Médoc
   Saint-Estèphe
   Pauillac
   Saint-Julien
   Margaux
   Moulis
   Listrac
Saint-Émilion
Pomerol
Côtes de Fronsac
Bourg

Blaye
Graves
Lussac-Saint-Émilion
Montagne-Saint-Émilion
Parsac-Saint-Émilion
Puisseguin-Saint-
   Émilion
Saint-Georges-Saint-
   Émilion
Sables-Saint-Émilion
Côtes de Castillon
Lalande de Pomerol

Well-Known Shippers of Bordeaux Wines

Barton & Guestier
Bouchard, Père et Fils
Calvet & Co.
Cordier
Cruse et Fils, Frères
Louis Eschenauer
Kressman & Co.
Sichel et Fils, Frères
Wildman & Fils

Médoc

The Médoc region produces most of the best known Bordeaux red wines. It is first divided into two sub-regions: Haut-Médoc and Bas-Médoc. Haut-Médoc, which is an Appellation Contrôlée, produces much better wines than Bas-Médoc, which is not an A.O.C.

Most of the wines from Haut-Médoc bear the names of its châteaux or its famous A.O.C. communes: Pauillac, Saint-Estèphe, Margaux, etc. The Médoc A.O.C. usually comes from the more northern Bas-Médoc.

Haut-Médoc wines are of high quality, varying from the full-bodied, fruity Saint-Estèphe wines to the lighter, softer Margaux, with Saint-Julien in between, and Pauillac offering some of the great big mellow wines of France: Château Lafite, Château Latour, etc.

Graves

Graves produces wines of both colors but is better known for its white wines, which are among France's finest full-bodied dry white wines. Its red wines can be excellent, and at their very best more expensive than the whites. They are not so delicate as Médoc reds, but they have remarkable clarity, good body, and bouquet. Château Haut-Brion, although a Graves, was classed in 1855 with the Médoc. A reclassification to-day might well include other red Graves as the peers of some of the great Médoc wines.

The white wines of Graves vary considerably. The area officially includes not only the sweet and luscious Sauternes but also Barsacs and Cérons, which moderate between the typical dry Graves and the sweet Sauternes.

Sauternes

Sauternes, although a part of the Graves region, produces unique white wine from five communes: Barsac, sold under its own name, and Sauterne, Bommes, Fargues and Preignac, sold as Sauternes. Although the region also produces some dry Sauterne (genuinely dry, not simply less sweet) and some red wine, only the golden sweet, high-alcohol white wine can be called Sauterne A.O.C. The red is almost never seen.

Barsac wines tend to be a little lighter and drier and perhaps owe more of their bouquet to the perfume of maturation than to the aroma of the Sémillon, Sauvignon Blanc, and Muscadelle grapes, from which they (like all Bordeaux white wines) are made.

Like the great German Trockenbeerenauslese, Sauternes are made from grapes picked when they are literally overripe and covered with noble rot, *Botrytis cinerea.*

The term Haut-Sauterne has no official meaning; it is used in the trade to designate a very sweet Sauterne.

Saint-Emilion

Saint-Émilion probably produces a greater quantity of excellent red wines than Médoc, but they often lack the delicacy of the great Médoc wines. They are also higher in alcohol, darker, and more full-bodied. At their most typical they seem to moderate between the classic Bordeaux wines and the Burgundies.

Although they are classed with other châteaux as First Great Growths, the Château Ausone and the Château Cheval-Blanc are outstanding. Both would rank with the best Médoc wines.

Pomerol

The crimson, full-bodied, velvety wines of Pomerol, adjoining Saint-Émilion, moderate between it and the Médocs. They have much of the fullness of the Saint-Émilion wines and much of the delicacy and mellowness of the Médocs. Pomerol contains only 1,500 acres, compared to the 16,000 of Saint-Émilion, and except for a few great châteaux (Pétrus, Certan-Giraud, Certan-de-May, Vieux-Château-Certan, La Conseillante, and Trotanoy) and some really excellent wine sold as Pomerol, it is not well represented.

Other Bordeaux Regions

Fronsac, next to Pomerol, produces red wines which resemble Pomerols, although they lack delicacy. Bourg and Blaye also produce quality red wines more in the Saint-Émilion family than the Médoc.

Entre-deux-Mers covers nearly 20 percent of the Bordeaux region. It produces large quantities of red and white wine. Quality and characteristics vary tremendously because of the size of the area. It includes numerous Appellations Contrôlées that have their own small reputations: Premières Côtes de Bordeaux for good white wines; Graves de Vayres for Graves-type wines; Loupiac for Sauterne-type whites; and Sainte-Croix-du-Mont for Barsac-type whites.

The wine sold as Entre-deux-Mers A.O.C. is white; the red wine is sold as Bordeaux A.O.C.

Burgundy

While the system of wine classification and nomenclature in Bordeaux is complex, it is orderly. A name on the label of a Bordeaux wine has a precise referent. Although obviously not every bottle called Pauillac A.O.C. will be like every other bottle, definite standards have been met by all bottles bearing the name, and the name itself is not misleading. A wine further defined as Château Latour is exactly that wine, no other, identical in all respects to every other bottle of that same year.

In Burgundy, the system of wine classification is not only complex but also confusing. Problems of nomenclature, resulting in a confusion of different wines or a puzzling difference in quality between bottles with the same name on the bottle, have four causes: (1) The vineyards in Burgundy are small, varying from miniscule to modest, and small proprietors of different vineyards sell their wines under the names of their villages, not their own names; (2) some vineyards have

numerous owners, each of whom independently produces his wine but legitimately and confusingly uses
the name of the vineyard; (3) the villages of the Burgundy region have taken the name of the most famous
vineyard in the region and attached it to their own;
(4) some vineyards also have the right to attach the
name of the most famous vineyard to their own.

These practices can make evaluation of Burgundy
wine based on past experience with them quite difficult. They also make a Bordeaux-style classification
system impossible. For example, the wine which bears
the name Chambertin (and no other qualifiers) is
among the most famous and excellent Burgundies. But
which Chambertin? The vineyard has 32 acres owned
by 25 people, each of whom produces his own Chambertin. Even if they were all equally skilled, and they
are not, their particular section of vineyard has its own
microclimate. Thus, there are at least 25 Chambertins.
There may be even more, as a shipper can buy several
Chambertins and make his own. In addition, because
of the reputation of the wine, the nearest village,
Gevrey, is called Gevrey-Chambertin, and there may
be as many as 10 or 12 vineyards (there could be
any number) who use the village name as their name.
Finally, there are vineyards in the locality which have
been given the right by the A.O.C. laws to attach
the name Chambertin to their own vineyard names:
Chambertin-Clos de Bèze, Ruchottes-Chambertin,
Chapelle-Chambertin, Mazoyères-Chambertin, and
others.

Short of learning about the wine by tasting it, the
purchaser might consider that the best wine is the one
that bears the name of a famous vineyard like Chambertin without qualification, shipped by a well-known
shipper. Next best are those that bear the vineyard
name, following with the wines that bear hyphenated
vineyard names, then those that bear village names
plus the words *premier cru*, and finally those that bear

only village names. The ranking of those bearing village names, the most frequent problem, must be on the basis of the reputation of the shipper or importer.

Major Growing Regions of Burgundy

The Burgundy production area is a narrow strip that extends about 130 miles. Until the nineteenth century, the entire area was cultivated, but after the phylloxera (vine-attacking plant lice) destroyed most French vineyards, only the best were replanted, and there is a gap of 40 or 50 miles in the production area.

The Basse-Bourgogne is comprised of the Côte d'Or, Côte Chalonnaise, Mâcennais, and Beaujolais growing areas.

The Côte d'Or, which produces the classic Burgundies, is further divided into the Côte de Dijon, the Côte de Nuits, and the Côte de Beaune. The production of the Côte de Dijon is limited and not extraordinary. The Côte de Nuit produces the most famous Burgundies (with the exception of Beaujolais), while the Côte de Beaune produces the most famous white Burgundies (with the exception of the Chablis, produced in the Yonne area, Haute-Bourgogne).

In essence, the Burgundies, as they are seen in the United States, consist of the production of Yonne, the Côte d'Or, the Côte de Nuit, the Côte de Beaune, and Beaujolais.

Major Appellations Contrôlées of Burgundy

Yonne and Côte d'Or

> Bourgogne
>
> Bourgogne-Aligoté
>
> Bourgogne Grand Ordinaire
>
> Bourgogne-Passe-Tour-Grains
>
> Bourgogne Mousseux

Yonne only

>Chablis Grand Cru
>Chablis Premier Cru
>Chablis
>Petit Chablis

Côte d'Or only

Bonnes-Mares[1]
Bourgogne Rosé
  Marsannay
Chambertin[1]
Chambertin-Clos de Bèze[1]
Chambolle-Musigny[2]
Chapelle-Chambertin[1]
Charmes-Chambertin[1]
Clos de la Roche[1]
Clos Saint-Denis[1]
Clos de Tarte[1]
Clos de Vougeot[1]
Côtes de Nuits
Échezeaux[1]
Fixin[2]
Gevrey-Chambertin[2]

Grands Échezeaux[1]
Griotte-Chambertin[1]
La Tâche[1]
Latricières-Chambertin[1]
Mazis-Chambertin[1]
Mazoyeres-Chambertin
Morey-Saint-Denis[2]
Musigny[1]
Nuits-Saint-Georges[2]
Richebourg[1]
Romanée[1]
Romanée-Conti[1]
Romanée-Saint-Vivant
Ruchottes-Chambertin
Vosne-Romanée[2]
Vougeot[2]

Côte de Beaune

Aloxe-Corton[2]
Auxey-Duresses[2]
Bâtard Montrachet
Beaune[2]
Bienvenue-Bâtard-
  Montrachet
Chassagne-Montrachet
Chevalier-Montrachet
Chorey-les-Beaune
Corton[1]
Corton-Charlemagne
Côtes de Beaune

Côtes de Beaune-
  Villages
Criots-Bâtard-
  Montrachet
Ladoix
Meursault-Blagny
Montrachet
Saint-Aubin
Saint-Romain
Santeny[2]
Savigny[2]
Volnay[2]

[1] Leading vineyards.
[2] Leading production areas.

Beaujolais

Beaujolais	Côte de Brouilly
Supérieur	Fleurie
Beaujolais-Villages	Juliénas
Brouilly	Morgon
Chénas	Moulin-à-Vent
Chiroubles	Saint-Amour

Côte Chalonnaise

Givry	Montagny
Mercurey	Rully

Mâconnais

Pouilly-Fuissé	Pouilly-Loché
	Pouilly-Vinzelles

Red Wines of Burgundy

There are two major "types" of Burgundy red wine: (1) the classic long-lived red Burgundies which are generally fuller, more velvety, more luscious, and more fruity than the Bordeaux wines, and (2) the popular short-lived, brilliant, light, fresh, vigorous, fruity Beaujolais.

The classic red wines come principally from the Côte d'Or region, specifically the Côte de Nuit. The Côte de Beaune contributes lighter wines which mature quickly. The leading wines might be listed as follows, although no official classification is possible: from Côte de Nuit, Romanée-Conti, Chambertin Clos-de-Bèze, Chambertin, Charmes-Chambertin, Clos de Vougeot, Richebourg, La Romanée, Romanée-Saint-Vivant, La Tâche, Musigny, Clos de Tarte, Bonnes Mares; from Côte de Beaune, Château Corton-Grancey, Corton, Corton-Bressandes, Corton Clos du Roi, and Aloxe-Corton.

Beaujolais wines differ substantially from the classic red Burgundies. They are made of Gamay grapes rather than Pinot Noir, and different soil and climatic conditions have influenced the wine dramatically. The producers of the best Beaujolais, although they may use the name Bourgogne, prefer to use the names of the nine vineyard areas listed in Table 7.7. The appearance of any of these names on a label indicates a potentially excellent wine. Those Beaujolais labeled *Beaujolais-Villages* are rated second and must come from one of 26 designated parishes or villages other than the nine most famous listed above: Brouilly, Chénas, Chiroubles. Beaujolais Supérieur may not be superior at all, and Beaujolais with no qualifier will never be more than a pleasant light wine.

White Burgundies

There are four distinct families of white Burgundy: Chablis, Montrachet, Meursault, and Pouilly. Chablis is the most famous, Montrachet the best.

Chablis is distinguished by a crisp, fresh taste that is favorably likened to the penetrating taste of metal touched with the tongue on a cold day. In great years, this flintiness is apparent in almost all Chablis, even the lesser growths. There are four qualities of Chablis: Chablis Grand Cru, Chablis Premier Cru, Chablis, and Petit Chablis. While the first three are qualities of essentially the same wine, Petit Chablis is much lighter and matures more rapidly. By law, all Chablis must be made from the Chardonnay grape. Chablis are not named after producing communes or villages, but the better ones are identified by the names of vineyards. Chablis were officially classified in 1936.

Chablis Classification

Grand Cru

> Blanchots
>
> Valmur
>
> Les Clos
>
> Grenouilles

Vaudésir

Les Preuses

Bougros

Premier Cru (in unofficial order of quality)

Montée de Tonnerre

Chapelot

Mont de Milieu

Vaulorent

Vaucoupin

Côte de Fontenay

Fourchaume

Les Forêts

Montmain

Butteaux

Vaillon

Beugnon

Séchet

Châtain

Côte de Léchet

Mélinots

Les Lys

Beauroy

Troëme

Vogros

Vogiras

The small vineyard of Montrachet produces France's most extraordinary white wine—luscious, elegant, full-bodied, yet delicate. Montrachet and the wines that have taken its name are slightly sweeter than Chablis. Bâtard-Montrachet and Chevalier-Montrachet adjoin Montrachet and resemble it. Other wines which merit the name are: Bienvenue-Bâtard-Montrachet, Criots-Bâtard-Montrachet, Les Caillerets (formerly Les Demoiselles), Les Combettes, and Les Folatières.

In addition to producing excellent red wines, Meursault produces green-white soft wines of quality, although less luscious than the Montrachet: Clos des Perrières, Les Perrières, Les Genevrières, Les Charmes, Les Santenots, and others.

Excellent white wines are also produced by the vineyard areas of Aloxe-Corton, which are somewhat overshadowed by the red wines of the same region: among the notable exceptions are Corton Charlemagne and Le Corton Blanc.

Mâconnais produces a number of notable white wines, but the most distinguished come from the

Pouilly (actually, the name of a hamlet), which offers Pouilly-Fuissé, Pouilly-Vinzelles, Solutré Pouilly, and Pouilly-Loché, but not Pouilly wines of the Loire Valley (discussed below). Distinguished growths include Les Pinces, Les Boutières, and Les Peloux. Most of this wine is seen as the golden, heady, rich Pouilly-Fuissé from the communes of Fuissé, Solutré, Chaintré, and Vergisson.

Shippers of Burgundy Wine

> Bouchard Père et Fils
> J. Calvert & Cie
> Chanson Père et Fils
> Cruse & Fils
> Louis Latour
> Patriarche Père & Fils
> Piat & Cie

Champagne

Champagne, the world's premier sparkling wine, is unusual in several respects. It is a white wine, but made from black and white grapes in the proportion of 4:1. It is purchased or classified not on the basis of communes, villages, or vineyards but by brand. Even in excellent years, it is legitimately a blend of several different vineyards' production and several different years.

Champagne is produced by about 200 firms; about 20 brands are imported into the United States. The major producing firms own vineyards or contract for the production of vineyards in various parts of the Champagne region in order to produce a wine that has qualities which will consistently be identified with the brand name.

Appellation Contrôlée laws, in addition to defining the Champagne (of French origin), have controlled its carbonation in the bottle. The law also regulates the production of vintage Champagne. It allows a shipper to blend some wine of other years into a bottle that will be labeled with a vintage year but prevents him from producing more "vintage" bottles by blending. Nor can he sell more than 80 percent of his production as vintage, whether he blends or does not, or ship before three years. In effect, these regulations and the general professional vigilance of an association of producers limit the possibility and the profitability of a single shipper fraudulently identifying a wine as a vintage. Vintage wines sell at considerable premiums.

In most years, Champagnes are all blends of good and ordinary years; they differ first by brand and then by the degree of sweetness. As the bottle is opened after the second (bottle) fermentation occurs, sugar syrup can be added in various quantities to produce Brut (very dry), Extra Sec (somewhat dry), Sec or Dry (somewhat sweet), Demi-Sec (sweet) or Doux (very sweet).

The taste for degrees of sweetness seems to be a national characteristic. Brut is favored by the English and American markets; the French prefer Extra Sec or Sec; and Latin Americans favor the most sweet. Presently, even Doux Champagne is only half as sweet as the Champagne sometimes offered 50 years ago.

While most Champagne is made from black and white grapes, by preventing any fermentation while the grape skins are mixed with the grape juice, pink Champagne can be made by allowing some alcohol from fermentation to dissolve the pigment in the black skins.

Champagne labeled Blanc de Blancs is made from white grapes only; it is usually lighter and drier and is labeled Brut.

Major Producer-Shippers of Champagne

Ayala	Laurent-Perrier
Bollinger[1]	Mercier[1]
Charles Heidsieck[1]	Mumm[1]
Heidsieck Monopole[1]	Perrier-Jouët
Krug	Pol Roger
Kunkelmann (as	
Piper-Heidsieck)[1]	Taittinger[1]
Lanson	Veuve Chicquot·
	Ponsardin

[1] Best-known leading shippers.

Rhône Valley

The Rhône Valley production area is unlike the other wine-producing regions of France. It extends from the Swiss border to the coast near Marseilles. A great deal of wine is produced, including some excellent red wines, some white wines, and some rosés. Part of the production is classified as Appellation Contrôlée, some as V.D.Q.S., but most of the production remains unclassified.

As the price of even the more general Burgundy and Bordeaux Appellation wines increases, wines labeled Côte du Rhône A.O.C. appear to be bargains. While they are not Burgundies or Bordeaux, the Côtes du Rhône are full-bodied, soft when mature, and quite flavorful.

The better wines of the region aspire to more than the simple Côte du Rhône A.O.C. Several are notable: Côte Rôtie, Châteauneuf-du-Pape, Hermitage, and Tavel.

Côte Rôtie

Côte Rôtie produces a fine full-bodied red wine, with deep color and the distinctive taste of the Syran, the dominant variety of the region. Only a small quantity is produced by all the vineyards in the Côte Rôtie area, and it is not readily available.

Châteauneuf-du-Pape

The Châteauneuf-du-Pape area is the most extensive region of the Rhône Valley. It produces over a million gallons of wine from a mixture of up to 13 different grape varieties. The wine is rich, full-bodied, crimson, and relatively high in alcohol (13 percent). Because numerous producers in the area are entitled to the Châteauneuf-du-Pape A.O.C., the name can be used for very different wines, blended of different grapes to the producer's taste. The best wines are produced by single estates: Domaine de la Nerthe, Domaine de Mont-Redon, Cabrières-les-Silex, Château Fortia, Domaine de Nayls, Saint-Patrice, and others.

Hermitage (Ermitage) and Crozes-Hermitage

Hermitage and Crozes-Hermitage are adjoining vineyard areas, producing both red and white wines. Although the wines are similar, the Hermitage area is better located, and the wine is a little better. Once these wines were thought to equal or exceed the best Bordeaux or claret, but they never fully recovered from the phylloxera infestation.

Certainly this full-bodied, dark, almost purple wine is the most famous of the Côte du Rhône. Unfortunately, production of both the red and the less notable white is limited. Most Hermitage is sold under that name, perhaps with a brand name or shipper's name on the label.

Tavel

Tavel, made from a mixture of grapes dominated by Grenache, is perhaps the best and certainly the most famous rosé wine of France. Similar pale, fruity rosé wines are also produced in Lirac and Chusclan.

Tavel wines have a brilliant color and a dryness that is unusual for a rosé. Most Tavel, in the Rhône Valley tradition, is sold by cooperatives, but some is available under vineyard names.

Condrieu

Condrieu is a less well known region of the Rhône Valley with its own A.O.C. Its most famous product is an excellent dry or semidry golden white wine. In some years, it is slightly sparkling. Limited production makes it a rarity outside of the Rhône.

Loire Valley

The vineyard area bordering the 600-mile-long Loire River is the longest growing area in France, and the least homogeneous. Vineyards are small, and their production varies in quality from mediocre to great. Interest in Loire wines is developing because their price has not yet skyrocketed; in the United States the names of the wines of the Loire are not yet household words like Burgundy, Beaujolais, Champagne, Côte du Rhône, Chablis, and Tavel of other regions. As the wines gain merited reputation, the price has increased. For example, the price of Muscadet, which can be enjoyed where Chablis might, has increased several-fold in the last few years.

There are four main Appellations Contrôlées, each with a clutch of other A.O.C. and some very good V.D.Q.S. associated with it. The name Loire is not an A.O.C., and since only 20 or 25 percent of the wines produced are of any gastronomic interest, this name alone on a bottle means little.

Anjou and Saumur

The west-central part of France produces three types of wine of note: (1) the sweet white dessert wines of Bonnezeaux, Coteaux du Layon, and Coteaux de la Loire, of which that of the Quart de Chaume is the best, most expensive, and most famous; (2) the Anjou rosés, and (3) the white wines of the Saumur. Some of the wine of the region is sparkling in varying degrees from lightly carbonated or *pétillant,* to wines with as much carbonation as Champagne. A good deal of the wine of this region is exported for the manufacture of sparkling wine in other countries.

Muscadet

The Appellation Contrôlée Muscadet refers to a grape, not to a particular growing region. Muscadet's dryness, flintiness, or crispness commends it to admirers of Chablis. The best are produced in the Coteaux de la Loire region of Anjou labeled as an A.O.C.; other producing regions surround the towns of Vallet, Clisson, Vertou, and Saint-Fiacre and bear the Appellation Contrôlée of Muscadet de Sèvre-et-Maine.

Touraine

Touraine has a larger production than Anjou and Saumur. In addition to producing wines which resemble the Anjou rosés and the Saumur whites, it offers the best reds to be found in the Loire: Bourgueil, Chinon, and Saint-Nicolas-de-Bourgueil, all A.O.C.

Vouvray is the most famous Appellation Contrôlée of Touraine. The wine sold under this name can vary from an almost sweet golden white wine to a sparkling wine quite resembling Champagne. While it must be produced in just eight communes to merit the A.O.C., other Appellations Contrôlées of the area usually resemble it in its best known form, slightly sparkling and crisp: Montlouis, Touraine-Mesland, Touraine Pétillant, and Touraine Mousseux.

Sancerre and Pouilly

Sancerre and Pouilly, vineyard areas on opposite sides of the Loire, are known for their quality flinty whites with great freshness and fruitiness. Among these, Pouilly-Fumé (A.O.C.) is the best known, both because of its quality and because of its long life and ability to travel well.

Alsace

Unlike the wines of other growing regions in France, wines from Alsace, on the French side of the Rhine, generally take their names from the grape used to produce them. Although there is some talk of organizing the classification of Alsatian wines in a way that offers more clarity, perhaps using the Burgundy system of hyphenated village and vineyard names, at the moment there is only one Appellation Contrôlée, Vin d'Alsace or Alsace. It always appears larger than the other names on the label.

When a wine from Alsace is labeled with the name of a grape, such as Riesling, the bottle must contain only wine from that grape. Production is subject to the A.O.C. laws and the wine statutes of the area interpreted by a committee of experts who determine the cultivation area, minimum amounts of grape sugar and alcohol, and the harvest date.

A wine containing a mixture of grapes is labeled *Zwicker* (blended) if it contains any grape varieties classified as ordinary, or *Edelzwicker* (finest blend) if it contains only noble varieties. Double names like Pinot-Traminer, which may appear in the literature, are no longer permitted.

Mass-Produced Ordinary Wine Grape Varieties

Chasselas and Sylvaner are widely planted in Alsace. The Chasselas is a light modest wine, white or rosé. It is seldom seen outside of Alsace. Sylvaner can be either ordinary or noble depending on the time of harvest (noble requires a late harvest). Most often, the ordinary Sylvaner is produced in the Bas-Rhin district, the lesser growing region of Alsace.

Knipperlé used to be more widely planted but has

now been replaced by Chasselas or the Müller-Thurgau, which resembles Chasselas, although it is a cross of Riesling and Sylvaner.

Noble Varieties

The white wines for which Alsace is known are produced from the Sylvaner, Traminer, Gewürztraminer (a development of Traminer), Riesling, Pinot Gris or Tokay d'Alsace, Pinot Blanc, and to a much lesser degree Muscat.

The Sylvaner is perhaps the least of the noble varieties. Wine from it is pleasantly acid, fruity, and sometimes slightly sparkling. Its strongest advocates describe it as "refreshing," which is hardly high praise. In all fairness, part of its lack of reputation is due to mass production in the Bas-Rhin. The Sylvaner from some areas can be good.

The Traminer or Gewürztraminer is the best known of the wines of Alsace. It is highly perfumed, flinty, and dry, but not acid. Traminer is less spicy— that is less highly aromatic—than Gewürztraminer (or *spicy* traminer).

Riesling is also well known and often more highly praised than Gewürztraminer for its full body, high alcohol content, delicacy, and aroma. In good years it undoubtedly produces the finest Alsatian wines.

The Tokay d'Alsace does not resemble the full-bodied, sweet Hungarian wines of the same name, but rather is a dry or semidry, mellow, slightly pink wine.

Pinot Blanc produced in Alsace is acid and full-bodied. Of all the noble varieties it is the least distinctive.

Alsatian Muscat, unlike other Muscat wines from southern Europe or California, is a dry, fruity, perfumed wine.

Alsatian Place Names and Vineyards

Some areas, villages, "sites," or vineyards have gained sufficient reputation to be important on the label. Also, because of the system of classification, the reputation of the shipper is important.

The most important areas of production are Thann, Riquewihr, Ribeauville, Bergheim, Hunawihr, Zellenberg, Mittelwihr, Kientzheim, Voegtlinshoffen, Ammerschwihr, Beblenheim, and Turckheim.

Some "sites" are important enough to stand alone without the name of the communal area: Rangen, Côte d'Olwiller, Kaefferkopf, Kanzlerberg, Schlossberg, Schoenenbourg, Sonnenglanz, and Florimont, among others.

Principal shippers include Leon Beyer, Domaines Dopff, Dopff & Irion, Theodore Faller, Jerome Lorentz, Metz Frères, and F. E. Trimbach.

Vins Délimités de Qualité Supérieure (V.D.Q.S.)

Southwest

Cahors	Irouléguy
Fronton	Côtes du Buzet
Côtes de Fronton	Vins de Lavilledieu
Villaudric	Côtes du Marmandais
Béarn	Vins du Tursan

Provence and the Rhone Valley

Châtillon-en-Diois	Coteaux de Pierrevert
Haut-Combat	Côtes de Provence
Côte du Luberon	Côtes du Vivaraise
Coteaux de Ventoux	Coteaux du Tricastin
Couteaux d'Aix	Coteaux d'Aix
	Coteaux des Baux

Savoy and Lyon Area

Vins de Savoie
Vins du Bugey
Vins du Lyonnais
Vins de Renaison Côte Roannaise
Côtes du Forez

Lorraine

Vins de la Moselle
Côtes de Toul

South of France

Corbières
Corbières Supérieures
Corbières du Roussillon
Corbières Supérieures
  du Rouissillon

Roussillon des Aspres
Minervois
Costières du Gard
Picpoule de Pinet

Languedoc

Coteaux de Véragues
Coteaux de Saint-Christol
Saint-Drézéry
Pic-Saint-Loup
Saint-Georges d'Orques
Cabrières

Saint-Saturnin
Montpeyroux
Faugères
Saint-Chinian
Coteaux de Méjanelle
La Clape
Quatorze

West-Central

Gros Plant de Pays
  Nantais
Coteaux d'Ancenis
Vins d'Auvergne
Côtes d'Auvergne
Vins de Saint-Pourçain-
  sur-Sioule

Vins de Orléanais
Coteaux du Giennois
Mont Pres (Chambord-
  Cour-Cheverny)
Coteaux de
  Chateaumeillant
Coteaux du Vendomois

8

Wines of Italy

In production of wine and in consumption of wine, Italy exceeds France. Unfortunately, neither in the quality of her wines nor the organization of her vineyards can Italy even begin to challenge France's leadership. The Italian Wine Law of 1963, Presidential Decree No. 93, passed to make production somewhat consistent with Common Market regulation, has the potential of offering the purchaser a classification and labeling system similar to the French Appellation Contrôlée scheme. At the moment, no one can begin to pretend to be able to systematically organize 1,500 different wines produced by thousands and thousands of small vineyards in a production area of 15,000 square miles.

Most of the wines, about 96 percent, are consumed in Italy. They are manufactured with the local market in mind and tend to offer vigor, roughness, and acidity rather than mature qualities of delicacy, smoothness, and bouquet. Few Italian wines are aged.

It is unlikely that consumers in the United States will ever see the majority of Italian wines. American vineyards produce ample quantities of similar ordinary table wines, some made from grapes of Italian origin by vintners of Italian origin, to make importation redundant and uneconomical.

The Italian wines worth noting are those which can now be described as fine and which have the possibility of becoming superb if the efforts of the government and professional associations (*consorzii*) are successful.

The law requires that wines be made from traditional, not hybrid vines. Production standards must conform to approved standards for planting, cultivation, fertilization, maximum allowed yields, maximum allowed residue, minimum alcoholic content, physical and chemical characteristics, as well as origin, if the wine is to be awarded the Denominazione di Origne Controllata (D.O.C.) or the more exacting Denominazione di Origine Controllata e Garantia. At this time the D.O.C. or the seal of a *consorzio* on a label means that the wine in the bottle is worthy of governmental or professional interest and is quite possibly excellent.

There are eleven major production areas:

1 Piedmont and Liguria
2 Lombardy
3 Veneto
4 Trentino-Alto Adige and Friuli-Venezia Giulia
5 Emilia-Romagna
6 Tuscany
7 Umbria and Latium
8 Marches
9 Abruzzi
10 Campania, Lucania, Apulia, and Calabria
11 Sicily and Sardinia

Piedmont and Liguria

Piedmont is the most famous Italian wine region; its production exceeds that of the United States and Russia combined. The Alps in the north provide natural protection from northerly winds, and vines flourish as far north as Susa and across the plains of Novara and Vercelli to the foothills of Monferrato.

Liguria faces the sea and lies directly to the south of Piedmont. It is better known for its seafood and fish than for its wine. Barbera wine is produced in the provinces of Asti and Cuneo and in the Monferrato area of Piedmont: Barbera d'Asti, Barbera d'Alba, and Barbera del Monferrato. These wines are made mainly from Barbera grapes. The wine from Asti and Alba is dark ruby when young, pomegranate when mature. Barbera del Monferrato is bright red and sometimes slightly sparkling.

Barolo wine is made in the Langhe hills south of Turin. It is produced only from Nebbiolo grapes. It has a rich bouquet of violets and roses, a bright ruby color, full body, and a relatively high alcohol content of 13 percent. Barolo matures in four years and is at its peak in about eight.

Barbaresco is similar to Barolo; it has slightly less alcohol and matures fully after three or four years. Gattinara and Carema, velvety, robust, pomegranate red, are also produced from Nebbiolo grapes. The Nebbiolo d'Alba dry wines are similar to them, but there is also a moderately sweet and a slightly sparkling Nebbiolo d'Alba.

Piedmont produces only one still white wine of real note: Cortese, a very pleasant straw-colored wine, with moderate alcohol and acid.

Asti Spumante, the Italian "Champagne," is also produced in Piedmont from the sweet Muscat grapes grown in the province of Asti. It is much sweeter than Champagne, not from added sugar syrup but from unfermented grape sugar.

The white wine of Liguria is probably better known than the red, especially Cinque Terre, a dry, slightly fragrant yellow to golden yellow sweet pleasant wine. Rossese, from the grapes of the same name, deep pomegranate red, dry, with 13 percent alcohol, is among the better Ligurian reds.

Lombardy

The wines of Lombardy are mostly made from the Barbera, Nebbiolo, and Croattina grapes. Oltrepo Pavese and the Valtellina are the major production areas.

Oltrepo red wines, made from Barbera and Croattina grapes, include the bright red slightly sweet Barbacarlo, the semi-sparkling, slightly bitter Sangue di Giuda, and the deep red, dry Buttafuoco. Four white varietal wines worthy of mention are also produced: light yellow, aromatic, pleasantly sweet Bonarda; light, dry, Pinot dell'Oltrepo Pavese; straw yellow, dry, full-bodied Riesling dell'Oltrepo Pavese; and Cortese, which is similar to Riesling but softer.

The wines of the Valtellina, produced largely from Nebbiolo grapes, are similar to the wines of Piedmont. Depending on the area where they are produced, they are called Sassella, Grumello, Inferna, and Valgella. All of them are a little sharp when young, growing softer with age until they are ruby red with a dry, full-bodied, well-balanced taste.

The red and rosé wines produced on the shores of Lake Garda are produced from Gropello, Sangiovese, Barbera, and Berzamini grapes. Both the red and the rosé are slightly bitter.

Veneto

Bardolina and Valpolicella are the most famous wines of the Veneto region. Bardolino, light red, brilliant, delicate, fresh, and smooth, is produced from several varieties of grapes near Verona. The ruby-red, more robust, slightly bitter Valpolicella is produced north of Verona in the Valpolicella and the Valpantena valleys, from the Corvino, Rondinella, and Molinara grapes.

Recioto Veronese is a special wine made in the same

area using only those grapes from the top and sides of the bunch, which are richer in sugar because they have received more sunlight. Alcohol content can reach 14 percent.

The province of Verona also produces Soave, one of Italy's finest white wines. It is produced from Garganega and Trebbiano grapes in about two dozen villages. Soave has a straw-yellow color, sometimes slightly green, a moderate alcoholic content, a mellow dryness, and a delightful aroma.

Trentino-Alto Adige and Friuli-Venezia Giulia

A great number of excellent wines are produced in the Trentino-Alto Adige and the Friuli-Venezia Giulia. At the moment they are better known in Europe, especially in Switzerland and Germany, than in the United States.

Four wines of the Trentino-Alto Adige merit attention—Santa Maddalena, Lago di Caldaro, Teroldego, and Terlano. Santa Maddalena is a superior red wine made from Schiavona, Schiave, and Lagrein grapes. It matures in one year and reaches its peak in two. The color becomes dark orange as it matures.

The ruby-red, soft, well-balanced Lago di Caldaro is another worthy red wine of the region. Teroldego has more alcohol than either Lago di Caldaro or Santa Maddalena. It is more robust when young, but gradually becomes smoother, while retaining its characteristic taste of almonds.

Terlano is the region's most famous white wine. It is produced from white Pinot grapes. Its original pale straw color with a greenish tinge changes to golden yellow when it matures.

The wines of Friuli-Venezia Giulia often have foreign varietal names like Cabernet, Cabernet-Sauvignon, and Tocai. Cabernet resembles its French cousins. White Cabernet-Sauvignon is straw yellow, high in alcohol, with a slightly bitter, warm taste and a delicate aroma.

Tocai is lemon yellow, dry, velvety, and mellow, unlike the Hungarian Tokay dessert wines.

Emilia-Romagna

Although Emilia-Romagna is among the largest Italian regions, it does not produce many wines which are famous in the United States. Only the red, slightly sparkling, sweet Lambrusco is really well known. The Lambruscos are named after areas of production, such as Lambrusco Salamino, Lambrusco Graspa Rossa, or Lambrusco di Sorbara. Another red wine, Sangiovese, is also worthy of note. Made from the Sangiovese grapes, it is deep ruby red with a purple tinge and has a dry, slightly bitter taste.

Only one quality white wine is made in Emilia-Romagna: Albana di Romagna, made from the Albana grapes from Bologna to Ravenna. There are dry, semi-sweet, and slightly sparkling versions. The dry Albana has a well-balanced, slightly acid taste; the others have a sweet, fruity flavor.

Tuscany

Chianti is Tuscany's and perhaps Italy's most famous wine. There are three different types, all produced from Sangiovese, Canaiolo, Malvasia, and Trebbiano grapes. Mass-produced Chianti, for local and Italian consumption, is made to be drunk young. It is low in alcohol, bright ruby red, dry, rough, and intense. The second type, exported in the flasks covered with straw, has been aged to acquire more body. It is garnet red and more perfumed. Lastly, there are the more full-bodied, well-aged Chiantis in bottles, with more alcohol, and a warm, exquisite taste.

Although the Chianti wines are produced over a wide region and bear the names of many areas—for example, Chianti Montalbano, Chianti Colli Fiorentini, Chianti Colli Pisane—the Chianti Classico region produces the best wines. Chianti Classico wines are identified by a rooster emblem on the neck of the bottle.

Vernaccia di San Gimignano, light golden yellow, dry, well balanced, bitter, is Tuscany's most famous white wine.

Umbria and Latium

Only two wines of Umbria are presently worthy of attention: the sweet or dry pale golden, delicate Orvieto and the greenish-yellow, dry, slightly astringent Trebbiano.

Latium to the south produces a number of good white wines. The pale yellow Est! Est! Est! of Montefiascone is well known for its amusing name and its inherent qualities. The dry version is full bodied.

The other wines of Latium are known as the Castelli Romani wines, of which each town has its own. The better known ones are Marino, Colli Albani, Frascati, and Torgiano. Frascati, made from Malvasia and Trebbiano grapes, is most famous; it is straw yellow, savory, soft and velvety. Marino, on the other hand, made from only Malvasia grapes, is more dry and fruity than Frascati. Colli Albani is dry or slightly sweet and has a noticeably fruity taste. Torgiano Bianco is also straw yellow with a slightly bitter but pleasant taste. Torgiano Rosso is ruby red, dry, well balanced, and full bodied.

Three generally good varietal wines are found in Latium: pale straw yellow, delicate Trebbiano, a dry rosé called Sangiovese, and a deep red, slightly bitter wine called Merlot.

Marches

Verdicchio dei Castelli di Jesi is the best known wine of the Marches region. It has a delicate, light straw yellow color with greenish glints and a dry, well-balanced taste with a slightly bitter aftertaste. Verdicchio made in the southernmost part of the region can be called Verdicchio Classico. Both are marketed in bottles shaped like ancient amphoras.

Two good red wines also produced in the Marches region are ruby-red, soft, full-bodied Rosso Conero and the similar Rosso Piceno.

Abruzzi

The Abruzzi region produces notable wine, from the Montepulciano grape. Montepulciano is ruby red with a pronounced dry taste and a pleasant aroma. After several years of aging, it acquires more body and mellowness.

Campania, Lucania, Apulia, and Calabria

The wines of the islands of Capri and Ischia are among the better known wines of Campania. Capri Bianco has a pale straw-yellow color and a dry, fresh, pleasant taste, with an alcohol content of about 13 percent.

Ischia produces a white and a red, full-bodied dry wine, as well as the ancient Falernum, presently called Falerno. The red Falerno is austere, full-bodied, and ruby red. The white is pale straw yellow with amber glints.

The mainland produces red and white Lacrima Christi. The white is pale straw with an amber tinge and has a well-balanced taste and subtle aroma. The red has deep ruby color, a dry taste and full bouquet.

The Apulia region produces a great quantity of red and white robust wine, much of which is blended or made into vermouth. Some effort has been made to sophisticate the wines. Sansevero, red, rosé, or white, for example, and Locorotondo have delicacy and quality.

Lucania has two well-known wines, an excellent full-bodied red wine called Aglianico del Vulture and a good sparkling dessert white wine called Malvasia del Vulture.

Calabria is famous for its Cirò. The original ruby-red color changes to dark orange when the wine is aged, and it loses its sweetish taste.

Sicily and Sardinia

The island of Sicily produces the well-known Marsala dessert wine, as well as a straw-colored fresh dry Etna Bianco and a ruby-red Etna Rosso that develops considerable quality when aged.

Sardinia is famous for its dessert wines but also produces a strong golden-yellow wine with a tart taste called Vernaccia di Oristano and a ruby-red Oliena, as well as full-bodied white Malvasia.

Checklist of Italian Wines

Piedmont

> *Asti Spumanti:* brilliant, straw color, delicate bouquet, fresh flavor, sparkling abundant foam
>
> *Barbaresco:* brilliant ruby red, delicate flavor, fragrant, dry, more mellow than Barolo
>
> *Barbera:* dark ruby red, full bodied, bouquet between cherry and violet
>
> *Barolo:* brilliant ruby red; after seven years takes on an orange brick color; bouquet of violets, and a resinous aftertaste
>
> *Bonarda:* dark ruby red, sometimes slightly sweet
>
> *Brachetto:* bright ruby red, pleasant bouquet, sweet and velvety; also sparkling version
>
> *Caluso (Passito di Caluso):* golden yellow or amber yellow; generous perfume, sweet and liqueur-like; rarely dry.

Chiaretto di Viverone: pinkish white, semidry, nutty

Cortese: pale straw yellow with green glints; delicate, tart

Fara: ruby, semidry

Freisa: deep purple, raspberry bouquet, sharp flavor; also sweet and sparkling

Gattinara: deep ruby red, astringent; but mellows with age

Grignolino: purple, clear, brilliant, nutty; mellows with age

Moscato d'Asti: straw colored, slight muscatel perfume, sweet, sparkling

Nebbiolo: light ruby red when young, orange-pink when mature; also sparkling; also rich ruby red like Barolo

Rosso Rubino di Viverone: ruby red, very dry

Vermouth di Turino: both red and white

Liguria

Cinque Terre: golden yellow, aromatic, delicate

Coronata: pale yellow, sweet or dry

Cortese di Liguria: straw yellow, dry, delicate

Dolceacqua: light ruby red, slightly sweet

Folcevera: light straw yellow, nutty, sweet; sometimes dry

Portofino: lemon yellow, dry taste

Sarticola: straw yellow, dry, distinctive

Vermentino Ligure: pale yellow, dry; sometimes slightly sparkling

Lombardy

Barbacarlo: strong red, delicate, mellow, soft, fruity

Buttafuoco: red, full bodied, lively

Chiaretto del Garda: pinkish, smell of almonds, nutty, dry

Frecciarossa: amber yellow, semidry, also dry white; also dry rosé; also ruby red

Inferno: deep ruby red, distinctive bouquet, soft

Moscato di Casteggio: pale, straw yellow, delicate, sweet; usually sparkling

Rosso Riviera del Garda: brilliant, light ruby, fruity, nutty, dry

Sangue di Giuda: dark red, nutty, sweet, sparkling; a little sharp

Sassella: ruby red, bouquet of roses, delicate

Tocai del Garda: brilliant, yellow-green

Villa: purple-red, very dry

Veneto

Barbarano: straw yellow, dry; also ruby, very dry

Bardolino: light ruby, light body, dry

Bianco di Conegliano: golden yellow, flinty, dry

Breganze: straw yellow, nutty, dry; also red, dry, slightly tart

Cabernet di Treviso: ruby red, full bodied

Cabernet Franc: ruby red, herbal bouquet, flinty

Gambellara: straw yellow, dry

Moscato di Arquà: dark yellow, aromatic, sweet

Prosecco: golden yellow, fruity, tart; also sparkling

Raboso: ruby red, delicate taste of cherries, tart, robust

Recioto Amarone: ruby red, dry, bitter aftertaste, robust

Soave: pale amber yellow, velvety, tart

Tocai: pale straw yellow, delicate, tart

Valpantena: ruby red, distinctive, dry, nutty

Valpolicella: dark ruby red, bitter almond taste

Verdiso: straw yellow, tart

Trentino-Alto Adige

Casteller: ruby, aromatic, well balanced

Castelli Mezzocorona: ruby red, dry, full bodied, well balanced

Eppaner Justiner-Appiano: red, dry, slightly bitter, full bodied

Lago di Caldaro: light garnet to brick red when aged, full bodied, mellow, well balanced

Nosiola: golden yellow, dry, full aroma

Santa Maddalena: dark ruby, well balanced, smooth

Terlano: brilliant, pale straw yellow, dry; fresh taste

Teroldego: violet red, bouquet of almonds and raspberries, matures dry, full bodied, intense

Friuli-Venezia-Giulia

Bianco del Colli: straw to golden yellow, dry, slightly sparkling

Bianco del Collio: straw yellow, dry

Merlot: deep ruby red, dry, smooth

Piccolit: deep straw yellow, sweet

Pinot: pale golden yellow, dry, tangy

Pinot grigio: straw yellow to gray-pink, sharp

Refosco: dry ruby, fruity, a little flinty

Sauvignon: straw yellow, tart

Terrano del Carso: bright red, nutty, raspberry bouquet

Tocai del Collio: lemon yellow, full bodied, dry

Tocai Friulano: lemon yellow to pale green, dry

Verduzzo: golden yellow, sweet

Emilia-Romagna

Albana: golden yellow, mellow, sweet; sometimes sparkling

Bianco di Scandiano: straw yellow, dry; also sweet; also sparkling

Lambrusco di Castelvetro: dark ruby red, violet bouquet, fruity, slightly sparkling

Lambrusco Grasparossa: very dark ruby red, violet bouquet, astringent, slightly sparkling

Lambrusco Salamino: ruby red, mellow, fruity, sparkling

Lambrusco di Sorbara: ruby red, violet bouquet, fruity, sparkling; dry or sweet

Sangiovese: dark ruby red, dry, tart

Trebbiano: straw yellow, dry; also slightly sweet

Tuscany

Aleatico di Portoferraio: deep ruby red, mild, aromatic, sweet

Ansonica: golden yellow, dry, nutty

Arbia: straw yellow, fine bouquet, dry, tart aftertaste

Bianco Vergine dei Colli Aretini: brilliant, light straw yellow, dry

Brunello di Montalcino: brilliant, purple red, violet bouquet, dry

Candia: straw yellow, sweet, aromatic; also red, full bodied, sweet

Chianti Classico: ruby red, mellow, light, tart, violet bouquet

Chianti Colli Aretini: ruby red, dry; often sparkling

Chianti Colli Fiorentini: ruby red, violet bouquet

Chianti Colli Senensi: light ruby red, mildly astringent

Chianti Colli Pisane: ruby red, rough

Chianti Montalliano: dark ruby, violet bouquet

Chianti Rufina: ruby red, nutty, sparkling

Moscatello di Montalcino: straw yellow, muscatel bouquet

Moscato d'Elba: brilliant golden yellow, full bodied

Procanico: pale, straw yellow, clear, bright, dry, delicate

Ugolino biserno: pale straw, dry

Vernaccia di San Gimignano: straw colored or golden, dry, tart aftertaste

Vino Nobile di Montepulciano: ruby red, dry, flinty, rough

Vino Santo Toscano: amber, or golden yellow, mellow

Umbria

Greco: amber, delicate, slightly sweet

Orvieto: pale golden yellow, dry, or semidry, tart aftertaste

Sacrantino: red, semidry, fruity

Latium

Aleatico di Gradoli: amber, mellow sweet, liqueur-like

Cannellino di Frascati: golden yellow, tart, dry or semidry

Cesanese: red, dry or semidry

Colli Albani: straw yellow, dry, slightly tart

Colli Lanuvini: golden yellow, full bodied, flinty

Est! Est! Est!: light yellow, dry or semidry

Falerno: straw colored, dry; also red

Grottaferrata: golden yellow, dry, slightly sharp

Malvasia di Grottaferrata: dark golden yellow, sweetish

Marino: golden yellow, slight tart aftertaste; dry or semidry

Montecompatri: golden yellow, dry

Moscato di Terracina: straw yellow, sweet, muscatel bouquet

Velletri: pale straw yellow, dry; also sweet; also red

Zagarolo: amber straw color, dry full bodied, flinty

Marches

Bianco Piceno: pale straw yellow, full bodied, tart

Montepulciano Piceno: brilliant dark ruby, dry

Rosso Montesanto: ruby red, fruity

Rosso Piceno: pale ruby, full bodied, tart

Verdicchio dei Castelli di Jesi: amber, straw yellow, dry or semidry

Abruzzi

Cerasuolo d'Abruzzo: cherry red, rough

Montepulciano d'Abruzzo: purple-red, fruity, nutty, strong

Trebbiano d'Abruzzo: dark golden yellow, dry

Campania

Aglianico: brilliant red purple, naturally sparkling

Asprino: clear straw yellow, tart

Biancolella: straw colored, aromatic

Capri: pale straw yellow, dry, full bodied; also red

Epomeo: straw yellow, dry, full bodied; also red

Falerno: straw colored, dry, delicate bouquet; also dry, fruity red

Forastera: straw yellow, dry, slightly sparkling

Gragnano: dark purple, nutty, dry

Ischia: straw yellow, greenish; also dry red

Lacrima Christi: straw yellow, dry, aromatic; also rosé; also red with bouquet of violets and almonds

Sanginella: golden straw yellow, sweet, slightly sparkling

Vesuvio: reddish purple, sparkling, full bodied, slightly astringent

Apulia

Aleatico di Puglia: dull red, mellow, sweet, aromatic, liqueur-like

Barletta: dark purple-red, heady

Castel del Monte: dark ruby red, dry, flinty; also dry white; also dry rosé

Malvasia Bianca: golden, sweet, soft, aromatic

Mistella: ruby red, orange, full

Moscato del Salento: golden yellow-amber, warm, smooth, mellow

Moscato di Trani: golden yellow, rose bouquet

Primitivo di Gioia: vivid red, sparkling, full bodied; also sweet

Rosato del Salento: reddish pink, dry

Torre Giulia: dark yellow, dry

Torre Quarto: purple-red, dry

Zagarese: dark ruby red, sweet flavor, delicate

Lucania

Aglianico del Vulture: purple red, fruity, naturally sparkling

Malvasia del Vulture: straw yellow, sparkling

Moscato del Vulture: straw yellow, sweet, sparkling

Calabria

Balbino d'Altromontone: straw yellow, fruity, liqueur-like

Cirò di Calabria: dark ruby red, lively flavor; also sweet

Greco di Gerace: golden yellow or amber, orange blossom bouquet

Lacrima: dark ruby, dry

Moscato di Consenza: amber yellow, sweet

Pellaro: red to pink, dry

Savuto: ruby, dry, smooth

Sicily

Albanello de Siracusa: golden yellow, dry, warm, full bodied, mellow, well aged

Capo Bianco: pale straw color, delicate, dry, smooth; also red Capo

Cerasuolo di Vittoria: cherry red when young, almost white after 30 years, full, dry, jasmine bouquet

Eloro: straw color, dry, baked taste; also red

Etna: greenish-white color, dry, delicate, well balanced; also rosé and red

Faro: bright ruby red, dry, well balanced, delicate bouquet of orange blossoms

Malvasia di Lipari: golden yellow, smooth, sweet, mellow, soft, well balanced

Mamertino: golden, dry or sweet

Marsala: golden yellow, sweet

Sardinia

Anghelu Ruju: ruby red, rich, full, sweetish cinnamon bouquet

Monica: ruby red to orange, delicate, smooth, warm, well balanced

Nasco: golden yellow, dry, slightly bitter, full bodied

Oliena: ruby red, dry, resinous, taste of strawberries

Vernaccia: golden yellow, dry, sweetish

Vermentino: pale straw, dry, slightly bitter, delicate

Shippers of Italian Wine

Marchesi L. & P. Antinori

Ansaldo Armando

Cantine Aurora

Casa Vinicola Bartelucci

Fratelli Beccaro

Arturo Bersano

Cav. G. B. Bertani

Luigi Bigi & Figlio

Luigi Bosca

Chianti Melini, S.p.a.

Fratelli Folonari S.p.a.

Gancia & C. S.p.a.

Palazzo al Bosco

I. L. Ruffino

Casa Vinicola Barone Ricasoli

Wines of Germany

Wine and the Law

The individual or the restaurateur purchasing German wines of the 1971 vintage in 1972 encountered a new labeling and classification system that has been designed to make identification simpler and to provide more quality control of German wines. It may take a decade or two to organize the nomenclature of German wines, but evident progress has been made in two important areas: (1) guarantee of origin and (2) quality identification and guarantee.

Until the new wine law, the only absolute guarantee of authenticity was an estate-labeled and estate-bottled wine. Geographical descriptions were extremely capricious. Wine might be labeled after any village within a certain area, so that in effect identical wine from the same vines might be called by different names. The present law divides Germany into wine-producing districts, and the districts into smaller areas called "Bereichs." The Bereich is composed of consolidated small vineyards, vineyards that alone do not meet the minimum acreage, and the individual vineyards which are sufficiently large. The consolidated vineyards are called "Grosslagen" and the individual vineyards are "Einzellagen." Consolidation has resulted in the elimination of over 25,000 names; this alone simplifies identification.

If a wine is now labeled with a village name—for example, Johannisberg—it must come from that village, not merely from the Johannisberg area. When the wine comes not from Johannisberg but from the general vicinity, it is labeled "Bereich Johannisberg."

When it comes from a Groslage consisting of the vineyards immediately bordering the village of Johannisberg—for example, the Groslage of Erntebringer—it is labeled with the name of the village and the name of the Groslage—in this instance, Johannisberger Erntebringer. When it comes from an individual vineyard within the village of Johannisberg—for example, Hölle—it is labeled with the name of the village and the name of the vineyard, in this instance Johannisberger Hölle.

The law also deals with quality, which depends on the weather, the location of the vineyard, and time of harvest. The quality of German wines is first dependent on their sugar content, which in turn depends on the amount of sunlight the grapes receive. The amount of sunlight depends on the weather in a particular growing season. It is said that a hundred days of sunlight make acceptable wine, but a hundred and twenty are necessary for great wines. After the weather, the location of the vineyard is important; position on a hillside determines how many hours of sun will be received. Location within a vineyard is also an important consideration, and the wines of the great estates in Germany are bottled from casks that correspond to different sections of the vineyard and different times of harvest. Unlike the producers of other regions, the grapes with the best qualities are not blended in vats with other grapes of the same vineyard to achieve a high middle standard. Excellent grapes are separated.

Besides weather and location, the time of harvest is a factor. The later a specific bunch of grapes is harvested, the more sugar it will have, both by greater exposure to the sun (hence more ripeness) and by the action of "noble rot," which intensifies sugar content.

When sugar content is not sufficient, for any one of these reasons, sugar is added so that the grape juice can be made into wine.

The law organizes these variables and documents them on the label, by grouping wines into quality classes that are dependent on chemical, physical, and the organoleptic qualities of the wine, not on geographical location. In other words, the same authentic geographical location, vineyard, consolidated vineyard, or subregion could produce—indeed would produce—wines of different qualities which would be so identified in the same year. The only remaining possible qualification is a cask number so that bottles from casks of different characteristics, which are from the same vineyard, in the same year, and of the same general quality, are identifiable.

There are three quality classes:

1   German table wine
2   German quality wine of designated regions
3   German quality wine with special attributes

German Table Wine (Deutscher Tafelwein)

Not much of this wine is exported, mainly because the difficulty of producing German wines by hand cultivation on precipitous slopes makes the lesser qualities too expensive to compete with inexpensive American and imported wines.

These table wines come from delineated areas and are made from approved grape varieties, mostly, like all German wines, Riesling and Sylvaner. The label shows the name of the region—for example, Moselle, Rhine, or Main—or the village but *not* a vineyard name.

Quality Wine of Designated Regions
(Qualitätswein bestimmter Anbaugebiete)

These wines are above average in quality, produced in designated regions from approved and suitable grape varieties. After the wine has passed a governmental analysis and tasting panel, it is given a control number which appears on the label. It must have reached a minimum alcoholic strength through natural sugar and must conform to the typical taste of the region and the grape. Quality wines must originate from certain geographic areas and may be named after a village or vineyard. Wines of this class always bear the words "Quality Wine" and show the control number on the label.

Quality Wines with Special Attributes
(Qualitätswein mit Prädikat)

These wines are of the highest classification. In addition to the labeling information for Quality Wines, different attributes are also indicated:

Kabinett (Cabinet) means that the wine is made only from fully matured grapes, without added sugar and from the harvest of a very limited district. This same word, Kabinett, will be seen on bottles produced before 1971, but at that time the word had no legal standing. Kabinett wines will have to pass more stringent standards than those same wines in the Quality Wine class.

Spätlese (late harvest) wines come from grapes which are picked after the completion of the normal harvest. They have, therefore, a higher degree of maturity and sugar, which means more flavor, fruitiness, and delicacy.

Auslese (selected harvest) wines are made from only the best bunches of grapes, selected and pressed separately. Some of the grapes have the noble rot, which results in a concentration of sugar and flavor.

Beerenauslese (berry selection) and *Trockenbeere-nauslese (dry berry selection)* have the highest degree of sugar concentration. Trockenbeerenauslese wines are made from grapes which have been left on the wood long enough to become near-raisins.

Every quality wine must list the bottler (Abfüller) and may list the producer. If the wine is bottled by the actual producer, who himself owns the vineyard, then the label says "Erzeugerabfullung" (bottled by the producer) and "aus eigenem Lesegut" (from his own grapes). Other terms and descriptions not covered by the law are no longer permissible, including such misleading information as geographical names that do not exist, pictures of mythical villages, or villages far from the production region.

German Wine-Producing Regions

Germany is not a very considerable producer or consumer of wine. There are only some 250 to 300 square miles of vineyards, compared with the thousands of France and Italy. The yield of quality wines per vineyard acre is the highest in the world, and German white wines, especially fine Rhine and Moselle wines, are unrivaled.

Most vineyards are planted on the steep hills that climb from major river valleys; specifically, the Rhine and its tributaries, the Nahe and the Main, and the Moselle and its tributaries, the Saar and the Ruwer.

The Rhine Region

The Rhine growing area consists of three major regions which are themselves divided into districts, villages, and vineyards. The regions are the Rheingau, Rheinhessen, and the Palatinate.

Rheingau, the best region of the Rhine, produces superior wines of considerable character, which need time to develop in the bottle. The wines of this region are unmistakable for their bouquet, freshness, and fineness. The village areas have achieved independent fame: Eltville, Erbach, Geisenheim, Hallgarten, Hattenheim, Hochheim, Johannisberg, Kiedrich, Östrich, Rauenthal, Rüdensheim, Winkel, and Kloster Eberbach. Individual vineyards are also famous; among them are Steinberg (Hattenheim), Schloss Johannisberg (Johannisberg), Baiken (Rauenthal), Schloss Vollrads (Winkler), and Doosberg (Östrich).

Rheinhessen is south of Rheingau, and produces fine, fruity, robust wines which are generally softer than Rheingau wines. Major villages include Oppenheim, Bingen, Büdesheim, Nackenheim, Nierstein, Worms, Norheim, Mönzingen, Niederhausen, Schloss Böckelheim, and Bad Kreuznach. Famous individual vineyards include Liebrauenstift (Worms), Sactrager (Oppenheim), Schlossberg (Bingen), and Rothenberg (Nackenheim).

Palatinate or Rheinpfalz is farther south than Rheinhessen, opposite French Alsace. It produces many of the very rich Beerenauslese and Trockenbeerenauslese wines because of its favorable southern location. In general, its wines are aromatic, rich, mellow, and big. The best-known village areas include Deidesheim, Bad Dürkheim, Forst, Königsbach, Ruppertsberg, Ungstein, and Wachenheim. Among the famous vineyards are Freundstück (Forst), Idig (Königsbach), and Frohnhof (Bad Dürkheim).

Two other regions can be included in the Rhine: Mittel Rhein (Middle Rhine), which produces full-bodied vigorous wines consumed locally; and the Baden and Württemberg production area on the river Neckar. Although Baden-Württemberg accounts for a fifth of the growing region, its considerable production is not generally of export quality.

The Rhine Tributaries Other Than The Moselle

The valleys of the Nahe and the Main rivers, tributaries of the Rhine, are also wine-producing regions.

The vineyards along the Nahe River produce a number of different wines, but the best known come from the middle Nahe about 15 miles from where it joins the Rhine at Bingen. The producing areas of Schloss Böckelheim, Mönzingend, Bad Kreuznach, Niederhausen, and Windesheim can be cited. The vineyards of Kupfergrube (Schloss Böckelheimer), Kahlenberg and Kronenberg (Bad Kreuznach) and Hermannshönle (Niederhausen) are well known.

The most famous wines of the vineyards along the Main River are grown near Würzberg in Franconia, about 80 miles from the confluence of the Main with the Rhine. They are known as Steinwein (the only wines of Franconia likely to be seen in the United States). Rather than the elongated Rhine or Moselle bottle, Steinwein is bottled in a flat green bottle called Bocksbeutel. The Sylvaner grape in the stony soil of this region produces a very firm wine.

The Moselle Region

The Moselle region is divided into three production areas: Obermosel, Mittelmosel, and Untermosel. Only the last two produce significant export wines.

Mittelmosel and Untermosel wines are light, elegant, delicate, refreshing, lively, and flowery. They do not age so well as the Rhine wines and are best consumed young.

Mittelmosel village vineyard areas include: Bernkastel, Brauneberg, Kues, Dhron, Enkirch, Erden, Graach, Neumagen, Piesport, Traben-Trarbach, Trittenheim, Ürzig, Wehlen, Wintrich, and Zeltingen. The most famous vineyards are: Sonnenuhr (Wehlen), Juffer (Brauneberg), Himmelreich and Josephshof (Graach), Goldtröpfchen (Piesport), Doctor (Bernkastel, Königsberg (Traben-Trarbach), and Würzgarten (Ürzig).

Untermosel village vineyard areas include Bruttig, Cochem, Pommern, Pünderich, Winningen, and

Zell. The most famous vineyards are Rathausberg (Bruttig), Schlossberg (Cochem), Kapellenberg (Pommern), and Hamm (Winningen).

Tributaries of the Moselle

The Saar and the Ruwer, tributaries of the Moselle, are known for wine. The best production of the Saar River vineyards is from the village vineyard areas of Ayl and Ockfen. The better known vineyards of the Ayl include Kupp, Herrenberg and Neuberg; those of Ockfen include Bockstein, Geisberg, Herrenberg, and Neuwies. In the Wiltingen area is Scharzhofberg, the most famous vineyard of the Saar.

Ruwer wines are known for their acidity and fine bouquet. They keep for two years—unusually long among Moselle wines. The villages of Avelsbach, Eitelsbach, and Mertesdorf are the best known. The most famous wine of the Ruwer is the Maximin-Grühauser Herrenberg (Mertesdorf), seconded by the Karthäuserhofberg (Eitelsbach) and Dom Herrenberg (Avelsbach).

Shippers of German Wine

Blum & Haas

G. B. Bohm

Nicola Clusserath

Arthur Hallgarten

Carl Jos. Hoch

Adolf Huber

Maximiner Stiftskellerei, Stephan Studert

Postholfkellerei GmbH

Reidemeister & Ulrichs

L. Rosenheim & Sons

Sichel Sohne Succ, Sichelonia Weinexport GmbH

Wilh. Wasum

Wines of the United States and Other Countries

France and Germany produce great wines. Italy produces fine wines and has the potential of producing great wines. No other country is likely ever to challenge them, partly because the expert and the consumer's definition of *great* includes characteristics unique to French, German, and Italian wines. Other countries produce pleasant, excellent, acceptable, satisfactory, decent, honest, or fairly priced wines. They should be purchased exactly on these bases, not because the consumer or the restaurateur expects a transcendent experience.

Yet Spain and Portugal produce specialty wines, such as Sherry and Port, which are unrivaled. Whatever France's reputation is for table wine, no one would seriously argue that French Sherry or Port approach the quality of the genuine wines.

In essence, the consumer and the restaurateur must have a purchasing perspective. There is a time for liverwurst and there is a time for foie gras; there is a time for denim and there is a time for vicuna.

Wines of the United States

To judge American wines fairly, the consumer and the restaurateur should attempt some objectivity in the midst of the exaggerated praise of patriot experts and producers and the unjustified wholesale disdain of foreign and domestic wine "snobs."

The United States does not produce any great wines. The grape varieties from which great European wines are made do not prosper or realize their full potential in the alien climate of the United States. In California, the largest of the 20 or more producing states, too much sun and too much fertility limit the possibilities for the quality of the European grape varieties.

On the other hand, the United States, especially California, produces inexpensive and medium-priced table wines that offer extremely good value. The American understanding of agriculture as a business, mass production with quality control, mechanized packaging, and mass distribution effect tremendous economies which at least in part are transmitted to the consumer. American jug wines, sold in gallons, with labeling that emphasizes the brand name of the producer, are universally better values than imported inexpensive wines. American bottled wines (with corks) provide medium-quality wines at moderate prices. They also offer individuality and personality when they are identified by growing region and varietal name; for example, Napa Valley Zinfandel.

The few producers of American wines with European pretension produce some medium-quality derivative wines. These are seldom good buys because the effort at imitation is costly beyond its potential quality return. Also, such wines are available in limited quantities, and it is impossible to consider them more than a curiosity.

The law in the United States is extremely rigid, but it is not consistent with the wine statutes of the European producers on the Common Market. An American wine labeled with the name of a grape must contain at least 51 percent wine from that grape. Names of foreign wines and foreign wine regions are not protected. Sherry, for example, must qualify by alcohol content, nothing else. Sauternes and Chablis are French growing regions, but in the United States, Sauterne and Chablis can be applied to any wine. It is legally possible, and indeed an occasional commercial practice, to draw Sauterne and Chablis from the same vat. There is little relation between the American wine and the European precursor, except when both are called by a varietal grape name like Riesling, Chardonnay, Traminer, Sauvignon Blanc, Barbera, Grenache, or Grignolino.

The more expensive American wines will be labeled with the name of a reputable vintner, a better growing region, and a grape variety. The less expensive American wines will be labeled to emphasize a brand name, which like that of most American products is meant to be assurance of consistent quality irrespective of season, harvest, or growing conditions of the raw materials.

California Wines

California produces 80 percent or more of American wine, about 160 million gallons, compared with 1,500 million gallons produced by Italy. About two-thirds of California's production is not table wine but fortified wine of poor or moderate quality.

Table Wine Varieties Three types of wine are produced: (1) varietal wines named after specific grapes; (2) generic wines named after European wine types; and (3) brand-name wines produced to conform with a commercial standard.

Varietal names are further qualified by the name of the vintner and the growing region (see below). The better red varietals include Cabernet Sauvignon, Pinot Noir, Gamay, Barbera, and Zinfandel. Notable white varietals are Chardonnay, Riesling, Sauvignon Blanc, Pinot Blanc, Chenin Blanc, and Traminer. Rosé varietals are best represented by Grenache, Grignolino, and Gamay.

Generic wines are named for the most famous European wines: Burgundy, Chablis, Sauterne, tokay, Chianti, Port, claret, Beaujolais, Tavel, Champagne, and sparkling Burgundy. The quality of the product varies enormously, since there is no control over the application of these names to California wines.

Brand-name wines are merchandised by both small and large concerns attempting to offer a marketable, accessible, consistent product. The wine may be a table wine or a refreshment wine bolstered with fruit juices and spices.

Major Growing Regions and Vineyards

Although some wine grapes are produced in most counties in California and sold to large vintners, there are three major production areas: the north coast near San Francisco, which is noted for its table wines, the interior valleys of the same region, and the Cucamonga district of Southern California, which produces fortified wines.

The north coast region can be divided into five production areas: Santa Clara-San Benito, Santa Cruz-Monterey, Livermore Valley-Alameda, Napa-Solano, and Sonoma-Mendocino.

The central area can be divided into three main districts, producing large quantities of cheap fortified wine: Lodi-Sacramento, Modesto-Ripon, Escalon and Fresno-San Joaquin.

Leading Northern California Wine Producers

Santa Clara-San Benito

Bertero Winery
Martin Ray Vineyards*
Paul Masson Champagne & Wine Cellars*
San Martin Vineyards
Almadén Vineyards*

Santa Cruz-Monterey

    Bargetto's Santa Cruz Winery

    Paul Masson Pinnacles Vineyard*

Livermore Valley-Alameda

    Weibel Champagne Vineyards*

    Wente Bros.*

    Concannon Vineyard*

Napa-Solano

    Beaulieu Vineyard*

    Beringer/Los Hermanos Vineyards*

    Christian Brothers Mont La Salle Vineyards and Winery*

    Inglenook*

    Louis Martini*

    C. Mondavi & Sons (Charles Krug Winery)*

    Robert Mondavi*

    Souverain Cellars*

Sonoma-Mendocino

    Cresta Blanca*

    Buena Vista Winery-Haraszthy Cellars*

    Italian Swiss Colony

    Korbel Champagne Cellars

    Sebastiani Vineyards*

* Produces varietals.

New York State Wines

The production of New York State (and the rest of the United States) is really insignificant, a few million gallons of fairly indifferent wine, distinguished only by the particular taste of the native American grape species and their hybrids.

The main growing region is the Finger Lakes of the

southwestern part of New York State, which in topography and exposure somewhat resembles the growing regions of the Rhine.

Numerous varietals are produced including Delaware, Catawba, Elvira, Isabella, Salem, Vergennes, and Riesling. The region also produces an assortment of fortified wines, Sherries, Ports, muscatels, and sweet dessert wines such as tokay and sweet catawba. In addition, sacramental and sparkling wines are produced.

The region's best efforts include such German derivative wines as Spätlese, Beerenauslese, and Trockenbeerenauslese. These might be tried before their prototypes as they are certainly representative of the type and less expensive than the German wines.

Other Wines of the World

A considerable list could be made of the countries which produce wine in large quantities, including South Africa, Australia, Holland, Malta, Crete, Greece, Hungary, U.S.S.R., and Algeria. Few of these wines are imported into the United States, and still fewer merit the effort. The best wines come from France, Germany, and Italy, and the United States produces an ample amount of ordinary wine, which leaves little room for the production of other countries.

Two markets for them exist: (1) the unfortunate consumer or restaurateur who has been misled into believing that production of a wine in some other country is somehow a guarantee of its quality or interest, and (2) the very few people who have an interest in high quality fortified wines, such as Port and Sherry.

Port

The immensely popular Port of California and New York only vaguely resembles the genuine quality Port of Portugal. A liking for one will not necessarily generate a liking for the other.

True Port is produced in a limited area of the Duoro Valley about 20 miles from Oporto in Portugal.

There are two main varieties of Port: red and white. The white, made from white grapes, is of negligible commercial importance and is being merchandised as an apéritif.

Red Port is the traditional Port. There are three main types: Vintage, Tawny, and Ruby, with a number of subdivisions.

Vintage Port is the wine of a single excellent year, bottled when it is between 18 months and two years old and allowed to mature 8 to 40 years in the bottle. Since this is necessarily an expensive process, there are several variations which accelerate or abbreviate the procedure.

Old Crusted Port is a blend of the wine of several years. It is left longer in the cask, thereby accelerating the maturation process, before being bottled and finished like Vintage Port.

Late Bottled Vintage Port has been kept in the cask for a protracted period, perhaps 10 or 15 years, then bottled, and given additional bottle age.

Tawny Port

Port which has been allowed to completely mature in the cask and is then bottled, usually as a blend, is called Tawny Port or Fine Old Tawny Port. Its age may exceed 20 years, and it is ready to drink when shipped. In fact, further aging may cause it to deteriorate.

Sometimes lesser wines are sold as Tawny Port when in fact they are relatively young blends of Ruby Ports and White Ports or Ruby Ports which have been partially decolored.

Ruby Port

Ruby Ports are kept in the cask until mature or almost mature, then bottled. They are the cheapest Ports but offer a freshness and vigor that may be more in keeping with modern tastes.

Ports, with the exception of Vintage Ports, are blends of several years, and they are usually purchased by the brand names of various shippers. These blenders attempt to develop an identity for their product. Among the better known shippers are: Cockburn, Smithes & Cia., Croft & Co., John Harvey & Sons, Robertson Bros., Sandeman & Co., and Silva & Cosens.

Sherry

Sherry wine is produced in the Jerez de la Frontera region of Andalucía, Spain. Because Sherry is always a blended wine, specific Sherries are identified by brand names or by the names of the shippers. When additional cases of a brand Sherry are needed, an order is sent to a supplier in Spain who prepares a new batch by blending wines of various years, vineyards, and qualities that he has stored in his warehouse (*bodega*) from butts grouped into *soleras*.

Sherries are made in various styles which may or may not be identified on the bottles.

Fino	very dry
Amontillado	less dry than Fino but still dry
Montilla	something like Amontillado, but may indicate that the wine is from only the wines of Montilla district
Manzanilla	the driest Sherry, often from the Sanlúcar de Barremeda region
Golden	medium sweet

Amoroso	sweet, usually inexpensive sherry
Brown	very sweet
Oloroso	full flavored, nutty, dry or sweet
Cream	blended from Fino and Oloroso
Milk	blended from Fino and Oloroso
Old East India	dark, brown Oloroso type

A number of the leading shippers' brands have become well known: Bristol Cream (Harvey); Dry Sack and Caruto (Williams & Humbert), Autumn Brown, Celebration Cream, Double Century, La Ina, Casino (Pedro Domecq), Rusa and Tio Pepe (Gonzales, Byass & Cia.), El Cid, and Royal Decree (Duff Gordon).